ACCRETION
THE GATHERING STORM

DIPAN KUMAR DAS
SUDIP KUMAR DAS

To all those who strive for a better world,

To the unsung heroes working tirelessly in the face of adversity,

To the leaders and innovators pushing the boundaries of what is possible,

To the communities who come together in times of crisis,

And to future generations, who will inherit the world we build today.

May this book serve as a guide and a call to action,

In the hope that together, we can overcome the challenges ahead

And forge a path towards a more resilient, just, and sustainable future.

Foreword

In an era defined by unprecedented change and complexity, our world faces a convergence of challenges that test the resilience of our societies, economies, and ecosystems. "Accretion: The Gathering Storm" delves into the pressing issues of our time, offering a comprehensive analysis of the multifaceted crises looming on the horizon.

The title itself, "Accretion," suggests a gradual buildup, a slow gathering of forces that, if left unchecked, will culminate in a storm of significant magnitude. This book seeks to explore the roots and ramifications of these accumulating pressures, drawing connections between disparate events and trends to present a cohesive narrative of our contemporary global predicament.

As you turn the pages, you will journey through the intricate landscape of environmental degradation, economic instability, political turbulence, social disintegration, and technological disruption. Each chapter meticulously dissects the underlying factors contributing to these crises, providing a clear-eyed assessment of where we stand and where we might be headed.

This book is not merely an exposition of problems. It is also a call to action, emphasizing the necessity for innovative thinking, collective effort, and transformative leadership. By examining case studies, historical patterns, and future scenarios, "Accretion: The Gathering Storm" aims to equip readers with the knowledge and insights needed to navigate the complexities of our time.

The issues addressed here are not confined to any one nation or region; they are global in scope and impact. As such, the solutions we seek must be equally expansive, rooted in a sense of shared responsibility and common purpose. The interdependence of our world means that the actions of individuals, communities, and nations are inextricably linked. Our response to these challenges will determine the trajectory of our future.

"Accretion: The Gathering Storm" is dedicated to those who envision a better world and are committed to making it a reality. It is my hope that this book will inspire you to engage deeply with the issues at hand, to think critically and creatively about solutions, and to join the growing movement of people working towards a more sustainable, equitable, and resilient future.

As you embark on this journey through the pages that follow, may you find both insight and inspiration, and may you be motivated to act with urgency and purpose. The gathering storm is upon us, but together, we have the power to navigate through it and emerge stronger on the other side.

Preface

The world we live in today is marked by complexity, interconnectedness, and rapid change. Every day, we are confronted with headlines about climate change, political instability, economic uncertainty, and technological disruption. It can be overwhelming to make sense of these issues, let alone find ways to address them. Yet, understanding the forces shaping our world is crucial for navigating the present and preparing for the future.

"Accretion: The Gathering Storm" was born out of a desire to explore the intricate web of challenges that define our time. This book aims to provide a comprehensive overview of the major crises facing our world, examining their root causes, interconnections, and potential solutions. It is an attempt to draw a coherent picture from the seemingly disparate events and trends that dominate our news cycles and daily lives.

The journey of writing this book has been both enlightening and sobering. As I delved into the research, I was struck by the magnitude of the issues we face and the urgency with which we must act. Yet, I was also inspired by the resilience, innovation, and determination of individuals and communities around the globe who are striving to make a difference. Their stories and efforts remind us that while the challenges are great, so too is our capacity for change.

Each chapter of this book addresses a different facet of the gathering storm: environmental degradation, economic instability, political turbulence, social disintegration, and technological disruption. These chapters are designed to stand alone, providing in-depth analysis and insights into each issue, but they are also interconnected, reflecting the reality that our world's problems do not exist in isolation. The interplay between these challenges creates a complex dynamic that requires holistic and integrated solutions.

Writing this book has reinforced my belief in the power of informed and engaged citizens. Our world is at a critical juncture, and the choices we make today will shape the future for generations to come. By understanding the nature of the challenges we face and the potential pathways forward, we can move from a state of reactive crisis management to proactive and transformative action.

"Accretion: The Gathering Storm" is not just a book for policymakers, academics, or activists; it is for anyone who cares about the future of our planet and our society. It is my hope that this book will spark conversations, inspire action, and contribute to a broader movement for positive change.

As you read through these pages, I encourage you to reflect on the role you can play in addressing the challenges we face. Whether through personal choices, community involvement, or broader advocacy, each of us has the power to contribute to a more sustainable, equitable, and resilient world. The storm is gathering, but together, we can chart a course towards a brighter future.

Thank you for embarking on this journey with me.

Prologue

The storm did not arrive suddenly. It has been building for decades, an accumulation of small changes and incremental pressures that, taken individually, might have seemed manageable. But now, as we stand on the precipice, the true magnitude of the challenges before us is coming into sharp relief. The forces at play are immense and intertwined, creating a complex and volatile global landscape that demands our immediate attention and action.

In many ways, the signs have always been there, for those who cared to look. The melting ice caps, the increasing frequency of natural disasters, the widening gap between rich and poor, the rise of authoritarianism, the erosion of trust in institutions, the rapid pace of technological change — all are harbingers of the storm that is now upon us. Each represents a facet of a larger, more insidious pattern of systemic fragility and interconnected crises.

This book, "Accretion: The Gathering Storm," is a call to awareness and a call to action. It seeks to illuminate the forces driving these global challenges, to unravel their complexities, and to propose pathways forward. It is an exploration of our present predicament and a guide to navigating the turbulent times ahead.

As you begin this journey through the pages that follow, you will encounter a detailed examination of the environmental, economic, political, social, and technological disruptions shaping our world. Each chapter delves into specific aspects of these broader categories, providing insights into their causes, impacts, and potential solutions. Together, they paint a comprehensive picture of the gathering storm.

Yet, this book is not merely an academic exercise in problem identification. It is imbued with a sense of urgency and a recognition of the power of human agency. While the challenges we face are formidable, they are not insurmountable. Through informed action, innovative thinking, and collective effort, we can mitigate the impacts of these crises and build a more resilient and sustainable future.

The prologue of this book sets the stage for what is to come. It is a reminder that the storm is both a crisis and an opportunity — a moment of profound risk and immense possibility. How we respond to this gathering storm will define our legacy and shape the world for generations to come.

As you read on, consider the interconnectedness of the issues discussed, the systemic nature of the challenges, and the necessity of holistic and integrated solutions. Reflect on the role that you, as an individual, can play in addressing these global crises. Whether through personal choices, community engagement, or broader advocacy, each of us has a part to play in navigating the storm and steering towards a brighter, more sustainable future.

The gathering storm is upon us. Let us face it with courage, determination, and a commitment to positive change. Welcome to "Accretion: The Gathering Storm."

Foreword

Preface

Prologue

1.

The Prelude To Crisis

2.

Environmental Challenges

3.

Economic Instabilities

4.

Political Turbulence

5.

Social Disintegration

6.

Technological Disruptions

7.

Global Health Threats

8.

Resource Scarcity

9.

Human Rights And Justice

10.

The Role Of Leadership

11.

Pathways To Resilience

12.

Conclusion And Call To Action

CHAPTER ONE

The Prelude to Crisis

Overview of the current global landscape

Economic Instability

The global economy is grappling with unprecedented challenges. Post-pandemic recovery has been uneven, with developed nations showing signs of growth while developing countries struggle to regain momentum. Inflation rates have soared, driven by supply chain disruptions, labor shortages, and rising energy costs. Central banks worldwide face the dilemma of tightening monetary policies to curb inflation without stifling economic growth. Meanwhile, debt levels in both public and private sectors have reached historic highs, raising concerns about potential financial crises.

Geopolitical Tensions

Geopolitical tensions are at their highest in decades. The rivalry between major powers such as the United States, China, and Russia has intensified, with conflicts over trade, technology, and territorial disputes. The war in Ukraine has had far-reaching consequences, straining international relations and destabilizing regional security. In Asia, tensions in the South China Sea and the Taiwan Strait threaten to escalate into open conflict, while the Middle East continues to be a hotbed of unrest and proxy wars.

Climate Change and Environmental Degradation

Climate change poses a critical threat to the global landscape. Extreme weather events, including hurricanes, wildfires, floods, and droughts, have become more frequent and severe, impacting millions of lives and causing billions in damages. Rising global temperatures and melting polar ice caps are leading to rising sea levels, threatening coastal communities and ecosystems. Efforts to combat climate change are hampered by political divisions and the slow transition to renewable energy sources.

Technological Disruption

Technological advancements are reshaping economies, societies, and daily life at an unprecedented pace. The rise of artificial intelligence, automation, and digitalization is transforming industries and labor markets, leading to both opportunities and challenges. While these technologies promise increased efficiency and innovation, they also raise concerns about job displacement, privacy, and cybersecurity. The digital divide between advanced and developing economies is widening, exacerbating inequalities.

Social and Political Unrest

Social and political unrest is on the rise globally. Widening inequality, perceived injustices, and erosion of trust in institutions have sparked protests and movements demanding change. In many countries, democratic norms are under threat, with increasing authoritarianism and populism. The COVID-19 pandemic has exacerbated these trends, highlighting disparities in healthcare, economic opportunities, and social services, leading to widespread discontent.

Health Crises

The COVID-19 pandemic has exposed the vulnerabilities of global health systems. While vaccination campaigns have made significant progress, new variants of the virus continue to emerge, threatening to prolong the health crisis. Beyond COVID-19, other health challenges persist, including the spread of infectious diseases, antibiotic resistance, and non-communicable diseases such as diabetes and heart disease. Global health inequities remain stark, with access to healthcare and medical resources varying dramatically between and within countries.

Migration and Humanitarian Crises

Migration and displacement are at record levels, driven by conflict, persecution, economic hardship, and climate change. Refugee crises in regions such as the Middle East, Africa, and Central America are placing immense strain on host countries and international organizations. The humanitarian needs of displaced populations are vast, including access to shelter, food, water, healthcare, and education. International cooperation is crucial but often hampered by political disagreements and resource constraints.

Conclusion

The current global landscape is characterized by complex and interconnected challenges. Economic instability, geopolitical tensions, climate change, technological disruption, social and political unrest, health crises, and migration are all contributing to a volatile and uncertain world. Addressing these issues requires coordinated international efforts, innovative solutions, and a commitment to sustainable and inclusive development. As the world stands at a crossroads, the actions taken today will shape the trajectory of the future.

Key indicators of impending crises

Economic Indicators

Rising Inflation Rates

Persistent increases in the cost of goods and services can erode purchasing power, decrease consumer spending, and strain household budgets.

High Debt Levels

Excessive public and private sector debt can lead to defaults, reduced investment, and financial instability.

Stock Market Volatility

Significant fluctuations in stock markets often signal underlying economic uncertainties or speculative bubbles.

Unemployment Rates

Rising unemployment can lead to decreased consumer spending, increased government spending on social services, and social unrest.

Currency Depreciation

Rapid devaluation of a country's currency can lead to inflation, increased cost of imports, and loss of investor confidence.

Geopolitical Indicators

Increased Military Activity

Escalation of military presence or actions in contested regions can signal impending conflicts.

Diplomatic Tensions

Deteriorating diplomatic relations, sanctions, and trade restrictions between countries can indicate rising geopolitical instability.

Political Instability

Governments facing significant internal opposition, protests, or coups can lead to national and regional instability.

Environmental Indicators

Extreme Weather Events

Increased frequency and severity of natural disasters like hurricanes, wildfires, floods, and droughts can signal environmental stress and impending humanitarian crises.

Climate Anomalies

Unusual climate patterns, such as prolonged heatwaves or unexpected snowfall, can indicate broader climatic shifts that impact agriculture, water supply, and ecosystems.

Social Indicators

Rising Inequality

Widening gaps between rich and poor can lead to social unrest, protests, and political instability.

Protests and Civil Unrest

Increased frequency and intensity of protests can indicate widespread dissatisfaction with government policies or socio-economic conditions.

Population Displacement

Large-scale movements of refugees and internally displaced persons can indicate conflict, persecution, or environmental degradation.

Health Indicators

Pandemic Outbreaks

The emergence and spread of infectious diseases can overwhelm health systems, disrupt economies, and lead to significant loss of life.

Health Infrastructure Strain

Overburdened healthcare facilities, shortages of medical supplies, and inadequate public health responses can signal an impending health crisis.

Nutritional Deficiencies

Widespread malnutrition and food insecurity can indicate systemic problems in food distribution and agricultural production.

Technological Indicators

Cybersecurity Breaches

Frequent and severe cyberattacks on critical infrastructure, financial systems, and government institutions can indicate vulnerability to technological crises.

Technological Unemployment

Rapid displacement of jobs due to automation and AI can lead to economic and social instability.

Migration and Humanitarian Indicators

Increased Refugee Flows

Significant increases in the number of refugees and asylum seekers can indicate conflicts, persecution, or environmental disasters.

Humanitarian Aid Needs

Rising demand for humanitarian aid and assistance in regions experiencing conflict, natural disasters, or economic collapse can indicate severe underlying crises.

Conclusion

Monitoring these key indicators can help policymakers, organizations, and individuals anticipate and respond to impending crises. Understanding the interconnected nature of these indicators is crucial for developing comprehensive strategies to mitigate risks and enhance resilience in the face of global challenges.

Historical precedents and patterns

Economic Crises

The Great Depression (1929)

Indicators: Stock market crash, bank failures, high unemployment, deflation.

Patterns: Over-speculation, excessive borrowing, and lack of regulation led to a severe economic downturn. The global nature of the crisis spread economic woes worldwide.

The Global Financial Crisis (2008)

Indicators: Housing market collapse, high default rates on subprime mortgages, credit crunch, bank bailouts.

Patterns: Excessive risk-taking by financial institutions, lack of transparency, and complex financial products led to a global recession. Government interventions were necessary to stabilize economies.

Geopolitical Crises

World War I (1914-1918)

Indicators: Rising nationalism, complex alliances, military buildups, regional conflicts.

Patterns: Tensions in Europe escalated into a global conflict after the assassination of Archduke Franz Ferdinand. The war reshaped international relations and borders.

Cold War (1947-1991)

Indicators: Ideological competition between the USA and USSR, nuclear arms race, proxy wars, espionage.

Patterns: Bipolar world order with frequent regional conflicts and political maneuvering. The Cold War ended with the dissolution of the Soviet Union.

Environmental Crises

The Dust Bowl (1930s)

Indicators: Severe drought, poor agricultural practices, massive dust storms.

Patterns: Environmental mismanagement and climatic conditions led to widespread crop failures and mass migration from affected areas in the United States.

Chernobyl Disaster (1986)

Indicators: Nuclear reactor explosion, radioactive contamination, health crises.

Patterns: Inadequate safety protocols and lack of immediate response exacerbated the disaster's impact, highlighting the risks of nuclear energy.

Social and Political Crises

The French Revolution (1789-1799)

Indicators: Economic hardship, social inequality, political corruption, Enlightenment ideas.

Patterns: Social unrest led to the overthrow of the monarchy, radical political changes, and widespread violence, including the Reign of Terror.

Arab Spring (2010-2012)

Indicators: Political corruption, economic issues, social media mobilization, public protests.

Patterns: A series of anti-government uprisings across the Arab world led to significant political changes, though outcomes varied widely by country.

Health Crises

Spanish Flu (1918-1919)

Indicators: Rapid spread of influenza, high mortality rates, overwhelmed health systems.

Patterns: A global pandemic with high mortality affected large populations shortly after World War I, exacerbating its impact.

HIV/AIDS Epidemic (1980s-Present)

Indicators: Emergence of a new virus, high infection rates, initially limited understanding and response.

Patterns: The epidemic highlighted the need for public health awareness, research, and international cooperation to manage health crises.

Technological Crises

Y2K Bug (1999-2000)

Indicators: Potential for widespread computer failures due to date programming issue, significant media attention.

Patterns: Extensive preventive measures averted major disruptions, showcasing the importance of early detection and intervention in technological threats.

Dot-com Bubble (2000)

Indicators: Overvaluation of tech companies, speculative investments, market correction.

Patterns: The burst of the bubble led to significant financial losses and a reevaluation of tech market valuations.

Migration and Humanitarian Crises

Syrian Refugee Crisis (2011-Present)

Indicators: Civil war, persecution, mass displacement.

Patterns: Millions of refugees fled to neighboring countries and Europe, highlighting the need for international humanitarian responses and the challenges of integrating displaced populations.

Rwandan Genocide (1994)

Indicators: Ethnic tensions, political instability, mass violence.

Patterns: The genocide led to a humanitarian crisis with millions displaced, highlighting the need for timely international intervention to prevent atrocities.

Conclusion

Historical precedents reveal patterns that can help anticipate and mitigate future crises. Economic, geopolitical, environmental, social, health, technological, and humanitarian crises often share common indicators and triggers. Understanding these patterns allows for better preparation and response, reducing the impact of future crises.

The role of globalization in shaping today's challenges

Economic Impact

Interconnected Markets

Benefit: Globalization has created a highly interconnected global economy where goods, services, capital, and labor flow across borders with relative ease, fostering economic growth and development.

Challenge: This interconnectedness also means that economic disruptions in one region can quickly ripple across the globe, as seen during the 2008 financial crisis and the COVID-19 pandemic.

Outsourcing and Job Displacement

Benefit: Companies can reduce costs by outsourcing production and services to countries with lower labor costs, leading to cheaper goods for consumers.

Challenge: This has led to job displacement in higher-cost countries, contributing to unemployment and social discontent, particularly in manufacturing sectors.

Wealth Inequality

Benefit: Globalization has lifted millions out of poverty, especially in developing countries, by providing new economic opportunities.

Challenge: It has also contributed to widening wealth inequality both within and between countries, as the benefits of globalization are unevenly distributed.

Geopolitical Tensions

Global Power Shifts

Benefit: Globalization has facilitated the rise of emerging economies, shifting the balance of global power and fostering multipolarity.

Challenge: This shift has led to increased geopolitical tensions, as established powers and rising nations vie for influence and control over global resources and strategic territories.

Transnational Issues

Benefit: Global cooperation has enabled collective action on transnational issues such as climate change, terrorism, and pandemics.

Challenge: Differing national interests and priorities can hinder effective global governance and cooperation, leading to fragmented and ineffective responses to global challenges.

Environmental Challenges

Resource Consumption and Environmental Degradation

Benefit: Globalization has driven technological advancements and efficiencies that can contribute to sustainable development.

Challenge: It has also led to increased resource consumption, deforestation, pollution, and greenhouse gas emissions, exacerbating environmental degradation and climate change.

Global Supply Chains

Benefit: Integrated global supply chains have enabled just-in-time production and reduced costs.

Challenge: These supply chains are vulnerable to disruptions from natural disasters, geopolitical conflicts, and pandemics, as seen during the COVID-19 crisis when shortages of critical goods occurred.

Social and Cultural Impacts

Cultural Exchange and Diversity

Benefit: Globalization has facilitated cultural exchange and diversity, enriching societies with new ideas, foods, music, and traditions.

Challenge: It can also lead to cultural homogenization and the erosion of local cultures and traditions, leading to identity crises and social tensions.

Migration and Urbanization

Benefit: Migration driven by globalization can fill labor shortages, contribute to economic growth, and foster multiculturalism in urban centers.

Challenge: Rapid urbanization and migration can strain infrastructure, social services, and lead to conflicts over resources and cultural integration.

Health and Safety

Global Health Collaboration

Benefit: Globalization has enabled international collaboration on health issues, including research, information sharing, and coordinated responses to pandemics.

Challenge: The ease of global travel and trade can facilitate the rapid spread of diseases, as seen with COVID-19, making global health security more challenging.

Safety Standards and Regulations

Benefit: Global trade agreements often include standards for product safety, environmental protection, and labor rights.

Challenge: Disparities in enforcement and regulations between countries can lead to exploitation, unsafe working conditions, and environmental harm.

Technological Advancement and Disruption

Innovation and Knowledge Sharing

Benefit: Globalization has accelerated technological innovation and the dissemination of knowledge, driving progress in various fields such as medicine, engineering, and information technology.

Challenge: Rapid technological changes can lead to job displacement, require constant skills upgrading, and create digital divides between those with and without access to technology.

Cybersecurity Risks

Benefit: Global connectivity has enabled unprecedented access to information and communication.

Challenge: It has also increased vulnerability to cyberattacks, data breaches, and misinformation, posing significant risks to individuals, businesses, and governments.

Conclusion

Globalization has been a powerful force for economic growth, cultural exchange, and technological progress, but it has also contributed to significant challenges. The interconnected nature of the globalized world means that issues such as economic instability, geopolitical tensions, environmental degradation, social inequality, health crises, and technological disruptions are often complex and interdependent. Addressing these challenges requires a coordinated global approach that balances the benefits of globalization with the need for sustainable and equitable development.

CHAPTER TWO

Environmental Challenges

Climate change and its global impact

Climate change is one of the most pressing issues facing the world today. It refers to long-term changes in temperature, precipitation, wind patterns, and other aspects of the Earth's climate system. These changes are primarily driven by human activities, particularly the burning of fossil fuels, deforestation, and industrial processes, which release greenhouse gases such as carbon dioxide and methane into the atmosphere.

Global Impacts of Climate Change

Environmental Impacts

Rising Temperatures: Global temperatures have risen significantly over the past century, leading to more frequent and severe heatwaves.

Melting Ice Caps and Glaciers: Polar ice caps and glaciers are melting at an accelerating rate, contributing to rising sea levels.

Sea Level Rise: Higher sea levels threaten coastal communities with flooding and erosion, potentially displacing millions of people.

Ocean Acidification: Increased CO_2 levels are causing the oceans to become more acidic, impacting marine life, particularly coral reefs and shellfish.

Changes in Precipitation Patterns: Altered rainfall patterns lead to more intense droughts and floods, affecting agriculture and water supply.

Ecological Impacts

Loss of Biodiversity: Many species are unable to adapt quickly enough to changing conditions, leading to extinction and loss of biodiversity.

Habitat Destruction: Changes in climate affect natural habitats, pushing species out of their traditional ranges and disrupting ecosystems.

Altered Migration Patterns: Many animal species are changing their migration patterns in response to shifting climates, which can affect breeding and feeding habits.

Human Impacts

Food Security: Changes in climate affect crop yields, threatening food security for millions of people, especially in vulnerable regions.

Water Scarcity: Altered precipitation patterns and melting glaciers impact water availability, leading to scarcity and potential conflicts over resources.

Health Risks: Rising temperatures and changing environments contribute to the spread of diseases, heat-related illnesses, and respiratory problems.

Economic Impacts: Climate change affects industries such as agriculture, fisheries, and tourism, leading to economic losses and increased costs for adaptation and mitigation.

Migration and Displacement: Environmental changes force people to leave their homes, leading to increased migration and potential conflicts in receiving areas.

Social and Political Impacts

Increased Inequality: Vulnerable populations, particularly in developing countries, are disproportionately affected by climate change, exacerbating existing inequalities.

Political Instability: Resource scarcity and displacement can lead to conflicts and political instability, affecting national and global security.

Climate Refugees: The concept of climate refugees is becoming more prominent as people are forced to migrate due to climate-related impacts.

Mitigation and Adaptation Strategies

Reducing Emissions: Transitioning to renewable energy sources, improving energy efficiency, and implementing carbon capture and storage technologies are crucial for reducing greenhouse gas emissions.

Sustainable Practices: Promoting sustainable agricultural, forestry, and land-use practices can help mitigate climate change and protect natural resources.

Resilient Infrastructure: Developing infrastructure that can withstand climate impacts, such as sea walls, flood defenses, and resilient buildings, is essential for adaptation.

International Cooperation: Global cooperation and agreements, such as the Paris Agreement, are vital for coordinating efforts to combat climate change.

Public Awareness and Education: Increasing public awareness and understanding of climate change can drive behavioral changes and support for policies aimed at mitigation and adaptation.

Climate change is a multifaceted challenge that requires urgent and coordinated action at local, national, and global levels. Addressing its impacts involves not only reducing greenhouse gas emissions but also developing adaptive strategies to protect communities and ecosystems from its inevitable effects.

Deforestation, biodiversity loss, and ecosystem collapse

Deforestation, biodiversity loss, and ecosystem collapse are interconnected environmental crises that have profound impacts on the planet and human societies. Understanding these issues and their interconnections is crucial for developing effective conservation and restoration strategies.

Deforestation

Causes of Deforestation

Agricultural Expansion: Clearing forests for crops and livestock is the primary driver of deforestation.

Logging: Commercial logging for timber, paper, and other forest products contributes significantly to forest loss.

Infrastructure Development: Building roads, highways, and urban areas leads to deforestation.

Mining: Extracting minerals and resources often requires large-scale clearing of forests.

Slash-and-Burn Agriculture: Traditional farming methods in some regions involve burning forests to create arable land.

Impacts of Deforestation

Climate Change: Trees absorb carbon dioxide; their removal releases stored carbon, contributing to global warming.

Loss of Biodiversity: Forests are home to a large proportion of the world's species;

deforestation destroys habitats and leads to species extinction.

Soil Degradation: Trees help maintain soil structure; their removal leads to erosion, nutrient loss, and decreased soil fertility.

Water Cycle Disruption: Forests play a critical role in the water cycle, affecting rainfall patterns and water availability.

Loss of Livelihoods: Indigenous and local communities often depend on forests for their livelihoods and cultural practices.

Biodiversity Loss

Causes of Biodiversity Loss

Habitat Destruction: Deforestation, urbanization, and agriculture reduce natural habitats.

Climate Change: Changing temperatures and weather patterns alter habitats and ecosystems.

Pollution: Chemical, plastic, and other pollutants harm wildlife and ecosystems.

Overexploitation: Overfishing, hunting, and harvesting of species beyond sustainable levels lead to population declines.

Invasive Species: Non-native species introduced to new environments can outcompete, prey on, or bring diseases to native species.

Impacts of Biodiversity Loss

Ecosystem Services: Biodiversity underpins ecosystem services such as pollination, water purification, and soil fertility.

Food Security: Many crops depend on pollinators and natural pest control provided by diverse ecosystems.

Health: Biodiversity contributes to medical research and provides compounds for pharmaceuticals.

Cultural and Recreational Value: Biodiversity enriches human culture and provides opportunities for recreation and tourism.

Resilience: Diverse ecosystems are more resilient to environmental changes and disturbances.

Ecosystem Collapse

Causes of Ecosystem Collapse

Deforestation: Removing forests disrupts ecosystems and can lead to their collapse.

Climate Change: Altered climate conditions can push ecosystems beyond their thresholds.

Pollution: Contamination of air, water, and soil can lead to ecosystem degradation.

Overexploitation: Unsustainable use of natural resources can deplete ecosystems.

Invasive Species: Invasive species can alter ecosystem dynamics and lead to collapse.

Impacts of Ecosystem Collapse

Loss of Ecosystem Services: Collapse leads to the loss of services that support human life and well-being.

Economic Consequences: Many industries, such as fisheries, agriculture, and tourism, depend on healthy ecosystems.

Human Displacement: Ecosystem collapse can force communities to migrate, leading to social and economic disruptions.

Biodiversity Loss: Collapsed ecosystems can no longer support their native species, leading to extinctions.

Cultural Impact: Many cultures have deep connections to their local ecosystems, and their collapse can erode cultural identities.

Strategies for Addressing Deforestation, Biodiversity Loss, and Ecosystem Collapse

Conservation and Restoration

Protected Areas: Establishing and effectively managing protected areas to conserve critical habitats.

Sustainable Practices: Promoting sustainable agriculture, forestry, and fishing practices to reduce environmental impact.

Restoration Projects: Implementing reforestation and habitat restoration projects to recover degraded ecosystems.

Wildlife Corridors: Creating corridors to connect fragmented habitats and support wildlife movement and genetic diversity.

Policy and Regulation

Environmental Legislation: Enforcing laws and regulations to protect natural areas and wildlife.

International Agreements: Supporting global treaties and conventions aimed at biodiversity conservation and climate change mitigation.

Indigenous Rights: Recognizing and upholding the rights of indigenous peoples to manage and protect their lands.

Education and Advocacy

Public Awareness: Raising awareness about the importance of biodiversity and the impacts of deforestation and ecosystem collapse.

Community Engagement: Involving local communities in conservation efforts and decision-making processes.

Research and Monitoring: Supporting scientific research to understand ecosystem dynamics and monitor changes over time.

Addressing deforestation, biodiversity loss, and ecosystem collapse requires coordinated efforts at local, national, and global levels. By implementing sustainable practices, protecting natural areas, and engaging communities, it is possible to mitigate these impacts and promote a healthier, more resilient planet.

Water scarcity and pollution

Water scarcity and pollution are critical issues that affect ecosystems, human health, and economic development worldwide. Both problems are exacerbated by climate change, population growth, and unsustainable practices, and they require comprehensive strategies for mitigation and management.

Water Scarcity

Causes of Water Scarcity

Climate Change: Altered precipitation patterns, increased evaporation rates, and more frequent and severe droughts reduce water availability.

Population Growth: Increasing population leads to higher water demand for domestic, agricultural, and industrial use.

Over-extraction: Excessive withdrawal of groundwater and surface water for irrigation, industry, and urban use depletes water sources.

Pollution: Contaminated water sources are unusable for drinking, agriculture, and industry.

Inefficient Water Use: Poor water management practices and outdated infrastructure lead to significant water loss and waste.

Impacts of Water Scarcity

Food Insecurity: Agriculture, which accounts for about 70% of global freshwater use, is heavily impacted, leading to reduced crop yields and food shortages.

Health Issues: Limited access to clean water contributes to the spread of waterborne diseases and poor sanitation.

Economic Consequences: Water scarcity affects industries, reduces economic productivity, and increases costs for water sourcing and management.

Social Conflicts: Competition for scarce water resources can lead to conflicts within and between communities and nations.

Environmental Degradation: Reduced water availability affects aquatic ecosystems, leading to loss of biodiversity and ecosystem services.

Water Pollution

Causes of Water Pollution

Industrial Discharges: Factories release pollutants such as heavy metals, chemicals, and toxins into water bodies.

Agricultural Runoff: Pesticides, fertilizers, and animal waste from agricultural activities contaminate water sources.

Urban Runoff: Stormwater runoff from cities carries pollutants like oil, heavy metals, and trash into rivers and lakes.

Sewage and Wastewater: Untreated or inadequately treated sewage and wastewater introduce pathogens and nutrients into water bodies.

Mining Activities: Mining operations release harmful substances such as arsenic and mercury into nearby water sources.

Impacts of Water Pollution

Human Health: Polluted water causes diseases such as cholera, dysentery, and hepatitis, posing significant health risks.

Ecosystem Damage: Pollution leads to the death of aquatic life, disrupts food chains, and damages habitats.

Economic Costs: Treating polluted water, health care expenses, and loss of tourism and fisheries revenue impose significant economic burdens.

Loss of Biodiversity: Contaminated water bodies cannot support diverse aquatic life, leading to reduced biodiversity.

Social and Cultural Impacts: Water pollution affects communities' access to clean water for drinking, bathing, and cultural practices.

Strategies for Addressing Water Scarcity and Pollution

Integrated Water Resource Management (IWRM)

Holistic Approach: Managing water resources in a comprehensive manner that considers all users and the sustainability of the ecosystem.

Stakeholder Involvement: Engaging local communities, industries, and governments in water management decisions.

Efficient Water Use: Promoting water-saving technologies and practices in agriculture, industry, and households.

Pollution Control and Prevention

Regulation and Enforcement: Implementing and enforcing laws to control industrial discharges, agricultural runoff, and wastewater treatment.

Green Infrastructure: Developing infrastructure that reduces pollution, such as wetlands for natural filtration and green roofs to manage stormwater.

Pollution Prevention: Encouraging practices that reduce the use of harmful substances and minimize waste generation.

Sustainable Practices and Technologies

Water Recycling and Reuse: Implementing systems to treat and reuse wastewater for irrigation, industrial processes, and even potable use.

Desalination: Using desalination technologies to convert seawater into freshwater, particularly in arid regions.

Rainwater Harvesting: Capturing and storing rainwater for use in agriculture, industry, and households.

Education and Awareness

Public Education: Raising awareness about the importance of water conservation and pollution prevention.

Capacity Building: Training local communities and industries in sustainable water management practices.

Research and Innovation: Supporting research into new technologies and methods for water conservation and pollution control.

International Cooperation

Transboundary Water Management: Collaborating on the management of shared water resources to ensure equitable use and conservation.

Global Agreements: Supporting international treaties and agreements that promote sustainable water use and pollution control.

Funding and Support: Providing financial and technical support to developing countries to improve their water management and pollution control capabilities.

Addressing water scarcity and pollution requires a coordinated effort at all levels of society, from local communities to international organizations. By implementing sustainable practices, enforcing regulations, and promoting education and innovation, it is possible to ensure the availability of clean water for future generations.

The rise in natural disasters and their socioeconomic effects

The rise in natural disasters and their socioeconomic effects is a significant concern globally, influenced by various factors including climate change, urbanization, and population growth. Natural disasters encompass a range of events such as hurricanes, floods, earthquakes, wildfires, and droughts, each posing unique challenges and impacts on societies.

Causes of the Rise in Natural Disasters

Climate Change

Increased Intensity and Frequency: Rising global temperatures contribute to more frequent and severe weather events such as hurricanes, heatwaves, and storms.

Changing Precipitation Patterns: Altered rainfall patterns lead to more intense and prolonged droughts or heavy rainfall, increasing the likelihood of floods and landslides.

Sea Level Rise: Melting ice caps and glaciers contribute to higher sea levels, exacerbating coastal flooding during storms.

Urbanization and Land Use Change

Population Growth: Increasing populations in urban areas and coastal regions expose more people and infrastructure to natural hazards.

Deforestation: Removal of natural vegetation reduces natural buffers against floods, landslides, and soil erosion.

Infrastructure Vulnerability: Poorly planned urban development and inadequate infrastructure increase vulnerability to disasters.

Geographical Factors

Tectonic Activity: Regions near tectonic plate boundaries are prone to earthquakes and volcanic eruptions.

Topography: Mountainous regions are susceptible to landslides and flash floods.

Wildfire Prone Areas: Dry and forested regions are at risk of wildfires, exacerbated by climate conditions and human activities.

Socioeconomic Effects of Natural Disasters

Economic Impact

Infrastructure Damage: Destruction of buildings, roads, bridges, and utilities requires extensive reconstruction and repair.

Loss of Livelihoods: Disruption to agriculture, fisheries, tourism, and other industries affects local economies.

Business Interruption: Closure of businesses and loss of productivity impact economic growth and stability.

Human Impact

Loss of Life: Natural disasters can result in fatalities and injuries, particularly in densely populated or vulnerable areas.

Displacement: Forced evacuation and displacement of communities lead to temporary or long-term relocation and humanitarian crises.

Health Risks: Increased exposure to waterborne diseases, injuries, and mental health issues among survivors.

Social Impact

Community Disruption: Disasters disrupt social networks, cultural practices, and community cohesion.

Vulnerability of Marginalized Groups: Disproportionate impacts on vulnerable populations such as the elderly, children, and people with disabilities.

Psychological Stress: Trauma and stress among survivors and rescue workers require mental health support and recovery efforts.

Strategies for Mitigation and Resilience

Disaster Preparedness and Response

Early Warning Systems: Implementing effective systems to forecast and alert communities about impending disasters.

Emergency Planning: Developing and testing emergency response plans at local, national, and international levels.

Search and Rescue: Training and equipping teams to respond swiftly to disaster-affected areas to save lives and provide immediate assistance.

Risk Reduction and Resilient Infrastructure

Building Codes: Enforcing stringent building codes and standards to ensure infrastructure resilience against natural hazards.

Green Infrastructure: Integrating natural and engineered systems to reduce flood risk, improve water management, and enhance urban resilience.

Land Use Planning: Implementing zoning regulations and land use policies to minimize exposure to natural hazards and protect critical ecosystems.

Climate Adaptation and Mitigation

Climate Resilience: Developing strategies to adapt to changing climate conditions and reduce vulnerability to extreme weather events.

Emission Reduction: Mitigating climate change through reducing greenhouse gas emissions to lessen the frequency and intensity of natural disasters.

International Cooperation: Collaborating on disaster risk reduction efforts, sharing knowledge, and supporting vulnerable countries in building resilience.

Community Engagement and Education

Public Awareness: Educating communities about disaster risks, preparedness measures, and evacuation procedures.

Capacity Building: Training local authorities, community leaders, and volunteers in disaster response and recovery.

Social Support: Providing psychosocial support, counseling services, and rebuilding community networks after disasters.

Addressing the rise in natural disasters and their socioeconomic effects requires a multi-faceted approach that integrates disaster risk reduction, climate adaptation, infrastructure resilience, and community empowerment. By investing in prevention, preparedness, and sustainable development practices, societies can reduce vulnerabilities and enhance resilience to natural hazards, ultimately mitigating their devastating impacts on economies, communities, and ecosystems.

Strategies for environmental sustainability and resilience

Strategies for environmental sustainability and resilience are crucial for ensuring that ecosystems can continue to provide essential services and support human well-being in the face of challenges like climate change and habitat loss. These strategies encompass a wide range of approaches aimed at conserving natural resources, reducing environmental impact, and fostering resilience in both natural and human systems.

Environmental Sustainability Strategies

Conservation of Natural Resources

Biodiversity Conservation: Protecting and restoring habitats to preserve biodiversity and ecosystem stability.

Sustainable Land Use: Promoting practices such as agroforestry and sustainable agriculture that maintain soil health and fertility.

Water Conservation: Implementing efficient irrigation techniques, promoting water-saving technologies, and reducing water wastage.

Energy Efficiency: Adopting energy-efficient technologies and practices to reduce greenhouse gas emissions and energy consumption.

Waste Management: Implementing reduce, reuse, and recycle principles to minimize waste generation and promote a circular economy.

Sustainable Development Practices

Green Infrastructure: Incorporating natural systems into urban planning to manage stormwater, improve air quality, and enhance biodiversity.

Smart Growth: Planning and designing cities and communities to minimize urban sprawl, preserve green spaces, and promote walkability and public transit.

Renewable Energy: Increasing the use of renewable energy sources such as solar, wind, and hydropower to reduce dependence on fossil fuels.

Carbon Footprint Reduction: Encouraging businesses and individuals to measure, manage, and reduce their carbon emissions through carbon offsetting and sustainable practices.

Corporate Sustainability: Adopting sustainable business practices that consider environmental, social, and governance (ESG) factors in decision-making and operations.

Resilience-Building Strategies

Ecosystem Resilience

Ecological Restoration: Rehabilitating degraded ecosystems through reforestation, wetland restoration, and habitat conservation.

Natural Resource Management: Sustainable management of fisheries, forestry, and agriculture to maintain ecosystem health and productivity.

Climate Adaptation: Developing strategies to help ecosystems adapt to climate change impacts such as sea level rise, temperature changes, and extreme weather events.

Community and Socioeconomic Resilience

Disaster Risk Reduction: Implementing early warning systems, emergency preparedness plans, and resilient infrastructure to minimize the impact of natural disasters.

Community Engagement: Engaging local communities in decision-making, capacity-building, and resilience-building efforts.

Livelihood Diversification: Supporting alternative livelihoods that reduce dependence on vulnerable resources and sectors.

Social Safety Nets: Establishing social support mechanisms, insurance programs, and financial instruments to help communities recover from environmental shocks.

Policy and Governance

Environmental Regulations: Enforcing and strengthening laws and regulations to protect natural resources, reduce pollution, and promote sustainable practices.

International Cooperation: Collaborating across borders to address global environmental challenges, share knowledge and resources, and support developing countries in building resilience.

Research and Innovation: Investing in scientific research, technology development, and innovation to advance sustainable practices, resilience strategies, and ecosystem management.

Education and Awareness

Environmental Education: Educating and raising awareness among the public, businesses, and policymakers about the importance of environmental sustainability and resilience.

Capacity Building: Providing training and technical assistance to enhance skills and knowledge in sustainable practices, resilience planning, and ecosystem management.

By integrating these strategies into policies, practices, and everyday decisions, societies can work towards achieving environmental sustainability and building resilience to ensure a healthy planet and prosperous future for generations to come.

CHAPTER THREE

Economic Instabilities

Global economic trends and vulnerabilities

Trends

Digital Transformation

Impact: Rapid advancements in technology are reshaping industries, business models, and consumer behavior globally.

Implications: Increased automation, AI integration, and digitalization are enhancing efficiency but also posing challenges such as job displacement and cybersecurity risks.

Shift in Global Economic Power

Impact: Emerging economies, particularly in Asia, are gaining prominence, reshaping global trade patterns and investment flows.

Implications: This shift presents opportunities for growth but also increases geopolitical tensions and competition for resources and markets.

Sustainability and Climate Action

Impact: Growing awareness of climate change is driving global efforts towards sustainable practices and renewable energy adoption.

Implications: Transitioning to a low-carbon economy requires significant investment and policy changes, impacting industries reliant on fossil fuels.

Demographic Changes

Impact: Aging populations in developed economies and youthful demographics in emerging markets are reshaping labor markets and consumer trends.

Implications: Challenges include pension obligations, healthcare costs, and adapting to changing workforce dynamics.

Trade Dynamics

Impact: Protectionist policies, trade tensions, and regional economic blocs are influencing global trade flows and supply chains.

Implications: Uncertainty in trade relations can disrupt economic stability, increase costs, and hinder global growth.

Vulnerabilities

Debt Levels

Issue: High levels of public and private debt in many countries, exacerbated by fiscal stimulus measures during the COVID-19 pandemic.

Risk: Rising interest rates could strain debt servicing capacity, leading to financial instability and potential defaults.

Financial Market Volatility

Issue: Stock market fluctuations and speculative bubbles in asset prices, fueled by easy monetary policies and investor sentiment.

Risk: Sudden corrections or market crashes could trigger broader economic downturns and undermine investor confidence.

Income Inequality

Issue: Widening wealth gaps between the affluent and lower-income groups within countries and globally.

Risk: Social unrest, reduced consumer spending, and political instability could result from disparities in income distribution.

Geopolitical Risks

Issue: Rising tensions between major powers, trade disputes, and regional conflicts.

Risk: Geopolitical instability can disrupt supply chains, increase energy prices, and hinder international cooperation on global issues.

Technological Disruptions

Issue: Cybersecurity threats, rapid technological advancements, and digital divides between nations.

Risk: Cyberattacks, data breaches, and technological unemployment could undermine economic resilience and trust in digital systems.

Environmental and Climate Risks

Issue: Climate change impacts, natural disasters, and environmental degradation.

Risk: Physical damages, resource scarcity, and regulatory changes could increase costs for businesses and governments, affecting economic stability.

Conclusion

Global economic trends indicate a landscape shaped by technological innovation, demographic shifts, sustainability imperatives, and evolving trade dynamics. However, vulnerabilities such as high debt levels, financial market volatility, income inequality, geopolitical tensions, technological disruptions, and environmental risks pose significant challenges. Addressing these vulnerabilities requires coordinated policy responses, international cooperation, and proactive measures to promote sustainable and inclusive economic growth in an increasingly interconnected world.

Income inequality and its repercussions

Definition and Measurement

Definition: Income inequality refers to the unequal distribution of income among individuals or households within a society.

Measurement: Typically measured using metrics such as the Gini coefficient, which quantifies the degree of income distribution inequality within a country or region.

Repercussions

Social Cohesion and Trust

Impact: High levels of income inequality can erode social cohesion and trust in institutions.

Repercussion: It can lead to increased social unrest, polarization, and a sense of injustice among disadvantaged groups.

Economic Growth and Stability

Impact: Extreme income inequality can hinder overall economic growth and stability.

Repercussion: It may limit economic mobility, reduce consumer spending, and create barriers to accessing education and opportunities for lower-income individuals.

Health and Well-being

Impact: Income inequality correlates with disparities in health outcomes and overall well-being.

Repercussion: Lower-income groups often face greater health risks, reduced access to healthcare services, and higher rates of chronic diseases and mortality.

Political Instability

Impact: Persistent income inequality can undermine political stability and democratic institutions.

Repercussion: It may lead to populist movements, policy gridlock, and challenges in addressing socio-economic issues through effective governance.

Education and Skills Development

Impact: Income inequality can limit access to quality education and skills development opportunities.

Repercussion: It perpetuates intergenerational cycles of poverty, reducing social mobility and economic opportunities for future generations.

Crime and Social Disruption

Impact: Income inequality is associated with higher crime rates and social disruptions.

Repercussion: It may strain law enforcement resources, increase incarceration rates, and exacerbate community tensions and safety concerns.

Causes

Globalization and Technological Advancements

Cause: Globalization and technological advancements have led to job polarization, where high-skilled workers benefit disproportionately compared to low-skilled workers.

Labor Market Dynamics

Cause: Changes in labor markets, such as outsourcing, automation, and declining unionization, contribute to wage stagnation and income disparities.

Policy and Taxation

Cause: Tax policies, social welfare programs, and regulatory frameworks can either mitigate or exacerbate income inequality based on their design and implementation.

Addressing Income Inequality

Policy Interventions

Education and Skills Training: Investing in education and lifelong learning opportunities to enhance human capital and promote equal access to economic opportunities.

Progressive Taxation: Implementing progressive tax policies and redistributive measures to reduce income disparities and fund social programs.

Labor Market Reforms: Promoting fair wages, worker rights, and job creation policies that support inclusive growth and reduce income gaps.

Social Safety Nets

Healthcare and Social Services: Ensuring universal access to healthcare, social services, and affordable housing to mitigate the impact of income inequality on health and well-being.

Promoting Economic Inclusion

Financial Inclusion: Expanding access to financial services and resources for marginalized communities to build assets and participate in economic activities.

Global Cooperation

International Development: Supporting global initiatives and partnerships to address systemic factors contributing to income inequality, such as trade policies and development assistance.

Conclusion

Income inequality is a complex socio-economic issue with profound repercussions for individuals, communities, and economies. Addressing its root causes and mitigating its effects requires comprehensive policy interventions, social reforms, and global cooperation to foster inclusive and sustainable economic growth. By promoting equitable access to opportunities, resources, and social protections, societies can work towards reducing income inequality and building more resilient and cohesive communities.

Debt crises in developed and developing nations

Definition and Causes

Definition: A debt crisis occurs when a country struggles to meet its debt obligations, leading to financial instability and potential default.

Causes:

Developed Nations:

Financial Sector Instability: Excessive leveraging and speculative investments in financial markets can lead to banking crises, as seen in the 2008 global financial crisis.

Sovereign Debt: High levels of government debt due to fiscal deficits, economic downturns, or unexpected expenditures can strain public finances.

Developing Nations:

External Debt: Heavy reliance on external borrowing from foreign lenders or international financial institutions to finance development projects or infrastructure.

Currency Depreciation: Vulnerability to currency fluctuations can increase the cost of servicing foreign-denominated debt, exacerbating debt burdens.

Political Instability: Weak governance, corruption, and inconsistent policies can undermine economic stability and investor confidence.

Impacts and Consequences

Economic Contraction

Developed Nations: A debt crisis can lead to recession, reduced consumer spending, and investment as credit tightens and confidence wanes.

Developing Nations: Economic growth can stagnate or decline, affecting employment, poverty levels, and overall development progress.

Financial Market Turbulence

Developed Nations: Financial market volatility can spread globally, affecting investor sentiment, stock markets, and currencies.

Developing Nations: Currency depreciation and capital flight can destabilize financial markets, leading to liquidity crises and banking sector instability.

Social Impact

Developed Nations: Austerity measures and cuts to social services can exacerbate income inequality, poverty, and social unrest.

Developing Nations: Reduced public spending on essential services such as healthcare and education can worsen living standards and social inequalities.

Political Instability

Developed Nations: Public discontent and political polarization can lead to electoral volatility and policy uncertainty.

Developing Nations: Political instability can undermine governance, deter foreign investment, and hinder economic reforms necessary for recovery.

Case Studies

Greece (Eurozone Debt Crisis, 2010-2018)

Causes: Excessive public debt, economic recession, and structural weaknesses in governance and taxation.

Impacts: Bailout programs, austerity measures, and social unrest strained economic recovery efforts and led to political turmoil.

Argentina (Debt Defaults, Various Periods)

Causes: Historical reliance on foreign debt, currency devaluations, and political instability.

Impacts: Periodic debt defaults, economic volatility, and social protests have hindered sustainable development and investor confidence.

Mitigation and Prevention Strategies

Financial Regulation and Oversight

Developed Nations: Strengthening regulatory frameworks for banks and financial institutions to prevent excessive risk-taking and speculative bubbles.

Developing Nations: Enhancing transparency, accountability, and governance to attract sustainable foreign investment and manage debt responsibly.

Debt Restructuring and Sustainability

Developed Nations: Implementing fiscal discipline, debt restructuring, and economic stimulus measures to promote recovery and growth.

Developing Nations: Negotiating favorable debt terms, diversifying funding sources, and investing in productive sectors to enhance debt sustainability and economic resilience.

International Cooperation and Assistance

Developed Nations: Supporting multilateral financial institutions in providing liquidity support and technical assistance to countries facing debt crises.

Developing Nations: Strengthening partnerships with donors, creditors, and international organizations to access development financing and promote inclusive growth.

Conclusion

Debt crises in both developed and developing nations highlight the vulnerabilities and interconnectedness of the global economy. Effective management and prevention of debt crises require proactive measures, sound economic policies, and international cooperation to ensure sustainable development, financial stability, and inclusive growth for all nations.

The impact of technology and automation on employment

Introduction

Technological advancements, particularly in automation and artificial intelligence (AI), have profoundly transformed the global labor market, reshaping job roles, skill requirements, and employment dynamics. While technology brings efficiency gains and innovation, its impact on employment is a subject of considerable debate and concern.

Positive Impacts

Increased Productivity

Benefit: Automation streamlines processes, reduces operational costs, and enhances productivity across industries.

Impact: This efficiency allows businesses to expand, create new job roles, and foster economic growth.

New Job Opportunities

Benefit: Technological advancements create demand for skilled workers in emerging fields such as AI, data science, cybersecurity, and digital marketing.

Impact: These roles often require advanced technical skills, leading to job creation in high-tech sectors and supporting industries.

Enhanced Safety and Quality

Benefit: Automation improves workplace safety by taking on hazardous tasks and ensures consistent product quality through precision manufacturing and monitoring.

Impact: Workers benefit from reduced injury risks and higher job satisfaction in safer environments.

Negative Impacts

Job Displacement

Challenge: Automation replaces routine, repetitive tasks traditionally performed by humans, leading to job losses in sectors like manufacturing, retail, and administration.

Impact: Workers without adaptable skills face unemployment or underemployment, contributing to income inequality and economic insecurity.

Skill Gaps and Structural Unemployment

Challenge: Technological advancements favor workers with specialized skills in STEM (Science, Technology, Engineering,

Mathematics) fields, leaving behind those with outdated skills.

Impact: Structural unemployment increases as displaced workers struggle to transition into new roles or retrain for tech-driven occupations.

Economic Inequality

Challenge: Automation widens the income gap between highly skilled workers benefiting from technological advancements and low-skilled workers displaced by automation.

Impact: Social disparities deepen as automation concentrates wealth and economic opportunities among a smaller, technologically savvy workforce.

Social and Psychological Effects

Challenge: Job insecurity and automation-related stress can lead to psychological distress among workers facing uncertain futures.

Impact: Communities reliant on industries susceptible to automation may experience social disruption, migration, and loss of local identity.

Mitigation Strategies

Investment in Education and Upskilling

Strategy: Promote lifelong learning programs, vocational training, and STEM education to equip workers with skills relevant to the digital economy.

Impact: Empower individuals to adapt to technological changes, pursue new career paths, and remain competitive in the job market.

Labor Market Policies and Regulations

Strategy: Implement policies that support workforce adaptation, such as job retraining initiatives, unemployment benefits, and labor protections.

Impact: Safeguard worker rights, mitigate job displacement impacts, and ensure fair transition opportunities in the face of automation.

Promotion of Inclusive Growth

Strategy: Foster inclusive economic policies that prioritize job creation in sectors less susceptible to automation, such as healthcare, education, green technologies, and creative industries.

Impact: Promote economic resilience, reduce income inequality, and support sustainable development in communities affected by technological disruptions.

Conclusion

The impact of technology and automation on employment is multifaceted, offering both opportunities and challenges for individuals, industries, and economies worldwide. While automation enhances productivity and innovation, it necessitates proactive measures to mitigate job displacement, address skill gaps, and promote inclusive growth. By investing in education, adopting flexible labor market policies, and fostering inclusive economic development, societies can harness technological advancements to create a more equitable and sustainable future of work.

Financial systems and the risk of collapse

Introduction

Financial systems play a crucial role in the economy by facilitating the flow of funds, allocating capital, and supporting economic growth. However, they are also susceptible to various risks that can lead to instability and, in severe cases, systemic collapse. Understanding these risks and their implications is essential for policymakers, regulators, and financial institutions to safeguard against potential crises.

Key Risks Leading to Financial Collapse

Liquidity Risk

Definition: Liquidity risk arises when financial institutions or markets cannot meet short-term obligations due to a shortage of liquid assets.

Impact: Inadequate liquidity can trigger panic withdrawals, liquidity spirals, and credit crunches, destabilizing financial markets and institutions.

Credit Risk

Definition: Credit risk refers to the likelihood of borrowers defaulting on their debt obligations.

Impact: Widespread defaults can impair the balance sheets of banks and investors, leading to asset write-downs, capital depletion, and financial distress.

Market Risk

Definition: Market risk encompasses fluctuations in asset prices, interest rates, exchange rates, and commodity prices.

Impact: Sharp market declines can erode investor confidence, trigger margin calls, and expose financial institutions to significant losses, especially in highly leveraged positions.

Systemic Risk

Definition: Systemic risk is the risk of widespread financial instability or collapse within the entire financial system, often triggered by interconnectedness and contagion effects.

Impact: Failure of a major financial institution or market disruption can propagate throughout the system, impairing financial intermediation and disrupting economic activity.

Operational Risk

Definition: Operational risk arises from internal failures, human error, inadequate systems, or external events.

Impact: Operational failures can lead to financial losses, reputational damage, and disruptions in critical financial services, undermining market confidence.

Contributing Factors to Financial Instability

Excessive Leverage

Factor: High levels of debt and leverage amplify risks during economic downturns or market corrections.

Impact: Leveraged positions increase vulnerability to liquidity shocks and exacerbate financial market volatility.

Complex Financial Instruments

Factor: Derivatives, structured products, and exotic financial instruments can obscure risk exposures and contagion pathways.

Impact: Mispricing or inadequate risk management of complex instruments can lead to unexpected losses and systemic disruptions.

Regulatory and Supervisory Weaknesses

Factor: Inadequate oversight, regulatory arbitrage, and lax enforcement of financial regulations.

Impact: Weak regulatory frameworks can foster risk-taking behavior, moral hazard, and systemic vulnerabilities within the financial system.

Global Interconnectedness

Factor: Cross-border capital flows, interconnected financial institutions, and international dependencies.

Impact: Contagion effects can transmit financial shocks across borders, amplifying systemic risks and complicating crisis management efforts.

Case Studies of Financial Crises

2008 Global Financial Crisis

Cause: Subprime mortgage market collapse, excessive risk-taking by financial institutions, and inadequate regulatory oversight.

Impact: Bank failures, credit crunch, economic recession, and widespread government interventions to stabilize financial markets.

Asian Financial Crisis (1997-1998)

Cause: Currency depreciation, unsustainable debt levels, and speculative attacks on Asian currencies.

Impact: Banking crises, economic contraction, and structural reforms to restore financial stability and investor confidence.

Mitigation Strategies and Resilience Building

Strengthening Financial Regulation

Strategy: Enhance prudential standards, risk management practices, and transparency requirements for financial institutions.

Impact: Promote sound financial intermediation, reduce systemic risks, and improve crisis preparedness.

Enhancing Supervisory Oversight

Strategy: Conduct rigorous supervision, stress testing, and scenario analysis to assess systemic risks and monitor market developments.

Impact: Early detection of vulnerabilities, timely intervention, and mitigation of risks to prevent financial crises.

Promoting Market Discipline

Strategy: Encourage market participants to adopt responsible lending practices, manage risk exposures prudently, and maintain adequate capital buffers.

Impact: Foster a resilient financial system that can withstand shocks, promote investor confidence, and support sustainable economic growth.

Conclusion

Financial systems are essential for economic prosperity but are inherently vulnerable to risks that can precipitate instability and collapse. By identifying key risks, addressing contributing factors, and implementing robust regulatory and supervisory frameworks, policymakers and financial institutions can mitigate systemic risks, enhance resilience, and safeguard against the recurrence of financial crises. Effective crisis management strategies and international cooperation are crucial in managing interconnected global financial markets and promoting sustainable financial stability in the long term.

CHAPTER FOUR
Political Turbulence

Rise of populism and authoritarianism

The rise of populism and authoritarianism is a complex global phenomenon with significant political, social, and economic implications. It involves the emergence of leaders and movements that challenge traditional political establishments and institutions, often appealing to the grievances and frustrations of marginalized or disaffected groups within society.

Factors Contributing to the Rise of Populism and Authoritarianism

Economic Inequality and Globalization

Income Disparities: Growing gaps between the wealthy and the rest of society can fuel resentment and distrust towards elites and established political systems.

Job Insecurity: Economic globalization and technological advancements have led to job losses and shifts, contributing to feelings of insecurity among workers.

Loss of Economic Sovereignty: Perceptions that international trade agreements and global economic policies undermine national sovereignty can foster nationalist sentiments.

Social and Cultural Factors

Identity Politics: Populist leaders often exploit divisions based on race, ethnicity, religion, or nationality to mobilize support.

Cultural Backlash: Resistance to progressive social changes, such as multiculturalism,

LGBTQ+ rights, and gender equality, can drive support for authoritarian leaders promising to protect traditional values.

Fear and Uncertainty: Events such as terrorism, immigration crises, and public health emergencies can amplify fears and increase support for leaders who promise security and stability.

Political Polarization and Distrust

Dissatisfaction with Establishment Politics: Perceptions of corruption, inefficiency, and a disconnect between political elites and ordinary citizens can erode trust in democratic institutions.

Media Fragmentation: Fragmented media landscapes and the spread of misinformation can reinforce echo chambers and polarize public discourse.

Weak Civic Institutions: Weak civil society, lack of independent media, and diminished civic engagement can undermine democratic norms and checks on executive power.

Impacts of Populism and Authoritarianism

Erosion of Democratic Values

Undermining of Rule of Law: Authoritarian leaders may weaken checks and balances, curtail press freedom, and suppress political opposition.

Democratic Erosion: Institutions such as the judiciary, electoral systems, and civil liberties may be weakened or manipulated to consolidate power.

Polarization: Political divisions deepen as rhetoric and policies exacerbate societal cleavages, leading to social unrest and instability.

Economic and Social Policies

Protectionist Policies: Populist governments may implement protectionist trade measures and economic nationalism, potentially leading to trade conflicts and economic instability.

Social Policies: Policies that target specific groups based on identity or economic status can exacerbate social inequalities and exclusion.

International Relations

Shifts in Diplomacy: Populist leaders may pursue isolationist or confrontational foreign policies, challenging international alliances and norms.

Global Governance: Weakening of support for multilateral institutions and global cooperation efforts can hinder responses to global challenges such as climate change and pandemics.

Responses and Challenges

Democratic Resilience

Strengthening Institutions: Upholding rule of law, reinforcing checks and balances, and safeguarding independent media and civil society are critical for protecting democratic norms.

Promoting Civic Education: Educating citizens about democratic principles, critical thinking, and media literacy can counter misinformation and promote informed civic engagement.

Supporting Democratic Movements: Providing international support to civil society organizations, human rights defenders, and independent media can bolster democratic resilience.

Addressing Root Causes

Economic Reforms: Implementing inclusive economic policies that address income inequality, job insecurity, and economic sovereignty concerns can reduce grievances that fuel populism.

Social Cohesion: Promoting inclusive societies that respect diversity and protect minority rights can mitigate identity-based divisions.

Political Dialogue: Fostering constructive political discourse, compromise, and consensus-building across ideological divides is essential for restoring trust in democratic processes.

International Cooperation

Global Solidarity: Strengthening international alliances and cooperation to defend democratic values, human rights, and the rule of law globally.

Normative Leadership: Exercising leadership on global challenges such as climate change, migration, and global health can reinforce the credibility of democratic governance models.

Addressing the rise of populism and authoritarianism requires a multi-dimensional approach that addresses economic, social, and political factors while upholding democratic values and institutions. By promoting inclusive governance, fostering social cohesion, and strengthening international cooperation, societies can work towards building resilient democracies capable of meeting the challenges of the 21st century.

Erosion of democratic institutions and norms

The erosion of democratic institutions and norms is a growing concern in many parts of the world, where democratic principles such as rule of law, separation of powers, electoral integrity, and respect for human rights are increasingly under pressure. This erosion can occur gradually through legislative changes, executive actions, or social shifts that undermine the foundations of democratic governance.

Factors Contributing to the Erosion of Democratic Institutions and Norms

Political Polarization

Divisive Politics: Increasing polarization and partisan gridlock can weaken consensus-building and cooperation necessary for democratic governance.

Us vs. Them Dynamics: Politicians and media framing issues in terms of "us versus them" can deepen societal divisions and undermine trust in democratic institutions.

Authoritarianism and Populism

Executive Overreach: Leaders may centralize power, weaken checks and balances, and bypass legislative oversight, concentrating authority in the executive branch.

Undermining Independent Institutions: Attempts to undermine the independence of judiciary, electoral commissions, and other oversight bodies can weaken their ability to hold governments accountable.

Media and Information Landscape

Misinformation and Disinformation: Spread of false information and conspiracy theories can undermine public trust in institutions and democratic processes.

Media Capture: Control or influence over media outlets by political interests can limit independent journalism and diversity of viewpoints.

Economic and Social Factors

Income Inequality: Growing disparities in wealth and opportunity can lead to perceptions of unfairness and disenchantment with democratic systems.

Social Unrest: Economic downturns, unemployment, and social unrest can increase support for authoritarian measures promising stability and security.

Global Trends

Erosion of International Norms: Shifts towards nationalism and isolationism in global politics can weaken support for international cooperation and norms of democracy and human rights.

Threats to Global Governance: Challenges such as climate change, pandemics, and migration can strain international institutions and lead to calls for more centralized control.

Impacts of Erosion of Democratic Institutions and Norms

Political Impact

Weakened Checks and Balances: Diminished independence of judiciary, legislative oversight, and media can lead to unchecked executive power.

Democratic Backsliding: Gradual erosion of democratic norms and institutions can lead to authoritarianism or illiberal governance.

Societal Impact

Loss of Civil Liberties: Restrictions on freedoms of speech, assembly, and association can stifle dissent and civic engagement.

Social Fragmentation: Divisions based on identity, ideology, or socioeconomic status can deepen, leading to societal unrest and polarization.

Economic Impact

Investment and Stability: Uncertainty and lack of rule of law can deter domestic and foreign investment, impacting economic growth and stability.

Corruption: Weakened institutions can facilitate corruption and cronyism, further undermining economic development and public trust.

Responses and Challenges

Strengthening Democratic Resilience

Reforming Electoral Systems: Ensuring free and fair elections, protecting electoral integrity, and promoting transparency in campaign finance.

Upholding Rule of Law: Protecting judicial independence, reinforcing constitutional checks and balances, and combating corruption.

Promoting Civic Education: Educating citizens about democratic principles, rights, and responsibilities to foster informed civic engagement.

International Cooperation

Support for Civil Society: Providing support to civil society organizations, human rights defenders, and independent media to strengthen democratic norms and accountability.

Diplomatic Pressure: Using diplomatic channels to advocate for human rights, rule of law, and democratic governance globally.

Global Norms and Standards: Upholding and promoting international norms and standards on democracy, human rights, and governance through multilateral institutions and agreements.

Public Engagement and Awareness

Media Literacy: Promoting media literacy and critical thinking skills to help individuals discern reliable information from misinformation.

Community Dialogues: Fostering inclusive dialogues and deliberative processes to build consensus and bridge societal divides.

Long-term Strategies

Institutional Reform: Undertaking reforms to strengthen democratic institutions, promote accountability, and restore public trust in governance.

Sustainable Development: Addressing underlying socioeconomic inequalities and promoting inclusive economic growth to reduce grievances and support democratic stability.

Addressing the erosion of democratic institutions and norms requires sustained efforts at local, national, and international levels to uphold democratic values, strengthen institutions, and promote inclusive governance. By protecting democratic freedoms, fostering civic engagement, and addressing underlying social and economic challenges, societies can work towards ensuring resilient and vibrant democracies for future generations.

Geopolitical tensions and conflicts

Geopolitical tensions and conflicts are a persistent feature of global politics, involving disputes and rivalries between nations or groups over territory, resources, ideology, or influence. These tensions can arise from historical grievances, geopolitical ambitions, competition for resources, or shifts in international power dynamics. Understanding their causes, impacts, and potential resolutions is crucial for managing and mitigating their effects on regional stability and international relations.

Causes of Geopolitical Tensions and Conflicts

Territorial Disputes

Border Disputes: Conflicts over territorial boundaries, often rooted in historical claims or demographic complexities.

Maritime Disputes: Competing claims over exclusive economic zones (EEZs), fishing rights, and access to strategic waterways.

Ideological and Religious Differences

Political Ideologies: Conflicts driven by ideological differences, such as democracy vs. authoritarianism, socialism vs. capitalism, or secularism vs. religious governance.

Religious Tensions: Conflicts rooted in religious differences, sectarianism, or competing claims over religious sites.

Resource Competition

Energy Resources: Competition over access to oil, natural gas, and other energy sources critical for economic development and geopolitical influence.

Water Resources: Disputes over shared water basins, exacerbated by increasing demand, climate change, and competing uses.

Geopolitical Rivalries

Regional Hegemony: Ambitions for regional dominance or influence, leading to proxy conflicts and geopolitical maneuvering.

Great Power Competition: Rivalry between major powers for strategic advantage, influence, and control over global affairs.

Historical and Cultural Factors

Colonial Legacy: Lingering tensions from colonial-era divisions, ethnic conflicts, or unresolved historical grievances.

Cultural Differences: Conflicts arising from cultural identities, language differences, or perceptions of national identity.

Impacts of Geopolitical Tensions and Conflicts

Humanitarian and Societal

Displacement and Refugees: Forced displacement of populations, refugee crises, and humanitarian emergencies.

Human Rights Violations: Violations of human rights, including atrocities, ethnic cleansing, and restrictions on freedoms.

Economic

Disruption of Trade and Investment: Economic sanctions, trade barriers, and instability impacting global markets and regional economies.

Infrastructure Damage: Destruction of infrastructure, hindering economic development and recovery efforts.

Political and Diplomatic

Diplomatic Isolation: Diplomatic fallout, severed ties, and strained international relations.

Security Threats: Escalation of military tensions, arms races, and proliferation of weapons.

Responses and Mitigation Strategies

Diplomatic Efforts

Dialogue and Negotiation: Engaging in diplomatic dialogue to de-escalate tensions, resolve disputes, and build trust.

Mediation and Conflict Resolution: Utilizing international mediation and conflict resolution mechanisms to facilitate peaceful settlements.

International Cooperation

Multilateral Diplomacy: Strengthening international organizations and alliances to promote cooperation, peacekeeping, and conflict prevention.

Sanctions and Diplomatic Pressure: Imposing targeted sanctions and diplomatic pressure to deter aggression and enforce international norms.

Conflict Prevention and Resolution

Early Warning Systems: Developing and implementing early warning systems to anticipate and mitigate potential conflicts.

Peacebuilding and Reconstruction: Supporting post-conflict reconstruction, institution-building, and reconciliation efforts.

Legal and Normative Frameworks

International Law: Upholding and promoting adherence to international law, treaties, and conventions governing conflict resolution and human rights.

Normative Standards: Promoting respect for human rights, democracy, and rule of law as foundational principles of international relations.

Public Engagement and Awareness

Civil Society Engagement: Supporting civil society organizations, grassroots initiatives, and peacebuilding efforts to foster dialogue and reconciliation.

Media and Information: Promoting responsible journalism, countering misinformation, and enhancing public understanding of geopolitical issues.

Addressing geopolitical tensions and conflicts requires a comprehensive and coordinated approach involving diplomatic efforts, conflict prevention strategies, international cooperation, and respect for international law and norms. By promoting dialogue, negotiation, and peaceful resolution of disputes, countries can contribute to regional stability, economic prosperity, and global peace.

The impact of misinformation and media manipulation

The impact of misinformation and media manipulation is profound and far-reaching, influencing public opinion, political discourse, and societal trust. Misinformation refers to false or misleading information spread unintentionally or deliberately, while media manipulation involves deliberate efforts to shape public perception through distorted or biased reporting or dissemination of information. Understanding these impacts is crucial in navigating today's media landscape and addressing the challenges posed by misinformation.

Impact on Society and Public Discourse

Erosion of Trust

Trust in Institutions: Misinformation undermines trust in traditional media, government institutions, and authoritative sources of information.

Social Cohesion: Divisive misinformation can exacerbate societal divisions along political, cultural, and ideological lines.

Polarization and Confirmation Bias

Echo Chambers: Misinformation reinforces pre-existing beliefs and biases, leading individuals to seek out and share information that confirms their views.

Polarization: Increased polarization in public opinion and political discourse as divergent narratives and "alternative facts" are promoted.

Political and Electoral Impact

Manipulation of Elections: Spread of false information and propaganda can influence voter behavior and electoral outcomes.

Undermining Democracy: Misinformation can erode democratic processes by distorting public debate and weakening informed decision-making.

Economic and Business Impact

Market Volatility

Financial Markets: False rumors and misinformation can lead to market volatility, affecting investor confidence and economic stability.

Consumer Behavior: Misinformation about products or services can influence consumer decisions and impact businesses' reputations.

Regulatory and Legal Challenges

Regulatory Compliance: Challenges for governments and platforms in regulating and combating misinformation while upholding freedom of expression.

Legal Liability: Liability concerns for media organizations and platforms regarding the spread of false or harmful information.

Health and Public Safety Impact

Public Health

Pandemics and Vaccines: Misinformation about health crises, treatments, and vaccines can undermine public health efforts and contribute to vaccine hesitancy.

Healthcare Decisions: Influence on individual healthcare decisions based on inaccurate or misleading health information.

Emergency Response

Disaster Response: Spread of false information during emergencies can hinder effective response efforts and exacerbate public panic.

Crisis Management: Challenges in managing misinformation during crises such as natural disasters or public health emergencies.

Strategies to Address Misinformation and Media Manipulation

Promoting Media Literacy

Education: Teaching critical thinking skills, digital literacy, and media literacy from an early age to empower individuals to evaluate information critically.

Fact-Checking: Encouraging fact-checking initiatives and promoting reliable sources of information to counter misinformation.

Strengthening Regulatory Frameworks

Transparency and Accountability: Requiring transparency in online advertising, algorithmic transparency, and accountability for platforms and media organizations.

Regulation: Developing regulations that balance freedom of expression with the responsibility to prevent the spread of harmful misinformation.

Collaboration and Partnerships

Public-Private Partnerships: Collaborating with tech companies, media outlets, civil society organizations, and researchers to develop effective strategies and tools.

International Cooperation: Promoting global cooperation to address cross-border misinformation challenges and share best practices.

Technology and Platform Interventions

Algorithmic Solutions: Adjusting algorithms to prioritize credible sources and reduce the spread of misinformation on digital platforms.

Content Moderation: Implementing content moderation policies and community standards to remove harmful content and disinformation.

Civic Engagement and Community Empowerment

Community-Based Initiatives: Supporting grassroots efforts, fact-checking organizations, and community-driven campaigns to promote accurate information.

Building Resilience: Empowering communities to recognize and resist misinformation through civic engagement and inclusive dialogue.

Addressing the impact of misinformation and media manipulation requires a multi-dimensional approach involving education, regulation, technological innovation, and collaboration across sectors. By promoting transparency, fostering critical thinking, and enhancing media literacy, societies can mitigate the harmful effects of misinformation and safeguard democratic processes, public health, and societal trust.

Strategies for political stability and governance reform

Strategies for achieving political stability and governance reform are essential for fostering effective, accountable, and inclusive governance systems that can respond to the needs of societies and promote long-term stability. These strategies encompass various approaches aimed at strengthening democratic institutions, promoting transparency, combating corruption, and enhancing civic engagement. Here are key strategies:

Strengthening Democratic Institutions

Rule of Law: Upholding the rule of law by ensuring equal treatment under the law, protecting human rights, and strengthening judicial independence.

Electoral Reform: Implementing electoral reforms to enhance transparency, fairness, and inclusiveness of electoral processes, including campaign finance regulations and voter education.

Parliamentary Oversight: Strengthening legislative oversight of the executive branch through robust parliamentary committees, accountability mechanisms, and checks and balances.

Decentralization: Promoting decentralization of governance to empower local authorities, enhance service delivery, and promote grassroots participation in decision-making.

Promoting Transparency and Accountability

Anti-Corruption Measures: Implementing comprehensive anti-corruption strategies, including enforcement of laws, establishment of anti-corruption agencies, and promotion of transparency in public procurement and financial transactions.

Open Government Initiatives: Adopting open government principles, such as open data policies, public access to information laws, and whistleblower protections to enhance transparency and accountability.

Independent Media: Ensuring a free and independent media sector that serves as a watchdog, promotes investigative journalism, and holds government officials accountable.

Civil Society Engagement: Fostering an enabling environment for civil society organizations, including freedom of association and expression, to engage in advocacy, monitoring, and oversight activities.

Building Inclusive and Responsive Governance

Public Sector Reform: Undertaking reforms to improve public sector efficiency, professionalism, and responsiveness to citizen needs, including merit-based recruitment and performance evaluation systems.

Social Dialogue: Promoting inclusive dialogue and consultation with diverse stakeholders, including marginalized groups, to ensure their voices are heard in policy-making processes.

Gender Equality: Implementing policies and programs to promote gender equality in governance and decision-making processes, including quotas and affirmative action measures.

Youth and Civic Education: Investing in civic education programs to promote civic engagement, democratic values, and participation among youth and future leaders.

Conflict Prevention and Resolution

Peacebuilding: Supporting conflict prevention initiatives, mediation efforts, and peacebuilding programs to address underlying grievances and promote reconciliation.

Dialogue and Reconciliation: Facilitating dialogue and reconciliation processes among communities affected by conflict or social divisions, fostering trust and social cohesion.

Security Sector Reform: Strengthening oversight and accountability mechanisms within security institutions to ensure they operate in accordance with human rights standards and serve the public interest.

International Cooperation and Support

Technical Assistance: Providing technical assistance and capacity-building support to strengthen governance institutions, promote legal and regulatory reforms, and enhance administrative capacity.

Diplomatic Engagement: Engaging in diplomatic efforts to support democratic governance, rule of law, and human rights internationally, including through multilateral organizations and partnerships.

Development Assistance: Aligning development assistance with governance reform priorities, including support for institutional strengthening, anti-corruption efforts, and democratic governance programs.

Long-term Sustainability and Monitoring

Sustainable Development Goals (SDGs): Integrating governance reform objectives into national development strategies and aligning them with the SDGs to ensure sustainable and inclusive development.

Monitoring and Evaluation: Establishing robust monitoring and evaluation frameworks to assess progress, measure impact, and adjust strategies as needed to achieve long-term political stability and governance reform.

By implementing these strategies in a coordinated and sustained manner, countries can strengthen their democratic institutions, enhance transparency and accountability, promote inclusive governance, and ultimately contribute to political stability, social cohesion, and sustainable development.

CHAPTER FIVE

Social Disintegration

Increasing social polarization and division

Social polarization refers to the deepening divisions within society along various lines, such as economic status, political ideology, cultural identity, and social values. This phenomenon is characterized by growing disparities, heightened social tensions, and a weakening sense of social cohesion. Understanding the factors contributing to increasing polarization is crucial for addressing its impacts and fostering greater societal unity.

Factors Contributing to Social Polarization

Economic Inequality

Cause: Widening wealth gaps between the affluent and disadvantaged groups.

Impact: Economic disparities can lead to social resentment, perceptions of unfairness, and reduced social mobility, exacerbating divisions within society.

Political Polarization

Cause: Increasing ideological differences and partisan divisions.

Impact: Polarized political discourse can foster mistrust, gridlock in governance, and undermine consensus-building efforts on critical societal issues.

Cultural and Identity Differences

Cause: Diverse cultural identities, beliefs, and values within multicultural societies.

Impact: Cultural divides can lead to social segregation, identity politics, and conflicts over cultural norms, traditions, and inclusion.

Technological Influences

Cause: Social media echo chambers, algorithmic biases, and misinformation.

Impact: Online polarization can reinforce ideological silos, amplify extremist views, and reduce exposure to diverse perspectives, fostering societal fragmentation.

Globalization and Economic Dislocation

Cause: Disruptions from globalization, job displacement, and socio-economic changes.

Impact: Global economic shifts can marginalize certain communities, fuel resentment towards global elites, and contribute to populist movements and nationalism.

Impacts of Increasing Social Polarization

Diminished Social Cohesion

Impact: Reduced trust and solidarity among diverse societal groups.

Consequence: Fragmented communities struggle to cooperate and address shared challenges, hindering collective progress and resilience.

Political Instability

Impact: Heightened social tensions and polarization in democratic systems.

Consequence: Erodes democratic norms, undermines political institutions, and increases susceptibility to populist rhetoric and authoritarianism.

Economic Inefficiency

Impact: Divisive social climates can deter investment, innovation, and economic growth.

Consequence: Stagnant economies fail to realize their full potential, exacerbating socio-economic inequalities and hindering upward mobility.

Social Fragmentation

Impact: Segmented societies experience isolation and marginalization of minority groups.

Consequence: Deepens social exclusion, exacerbates discrimination, and undermines efforts towards social justice and equality.

Mitigating Social Polarization

Promoting Inclusive Economic Growth

Strategy: Addressing economic disparities through progressive taxation, social safety nets, and inclusive economic policies.

Impact: Reducing inequality can enhance social mobility, foster a sense of fairness, and promote societal cohesion.

Strengthening Civic Engagement

Strategy: Encouraging civil discourse, civic education, and community involvement.

Impact: Empowering citizens to participate in democratic processes, bridge divides, and build consensus on shared values and priorities.

Regulating Technology and Media

Strategy: Promoting media literacy, transparency in algorithms, and ethical standards in digital platforms.

Impact: Mitigating misinformation, fostering diverse viewpoints, and promoting informed public discourse.

Fostering Intercultural Understanding

Strategy: Encouraging dialogue, cultural exchange, and respect for diversity.

Impact: Building bridges across cultural divides, promoting tolerance, and cultivating a sense of national unity amidst diversity.

Conclusion

Addressing increasing social polarization requires proactive measures to mitigate economic disparities, foster inclusive social policies, and promote civic engagement and dialogue across diverse communities. By addressing root causes, promoting unity amidst diversity, and strengthening social cohesion, societies can build resilience, enhance democratic stability, and achieve sustainable progress towards a more equitable and harmonious future.

The impact of cultural and identity politics

Cultural and identity politics refer to the mobilization of cultural, ethnic, racial, gender, or other identity-based identities as a basis for political action and advocacy. This phenomenon has significant implications for social cohesion, policy-making, and societal values, often shaping public discourse and influencing political landscapes.

Key Impacts of Cultural and Identity Politics

Empowerment of Marginalized Groups

Impact: Cultural and identity politics empower marginalized communities to assert their rights, advocate for social justice, and challenge systemic inequalities.

Example: Movements advocating for civil rights, LGBTQ+ rights, indigenous rights, and gender equality have brought visibility to marginalized voices and influenced policy reforms.

Polarization and Divisiveness

Impact: Identity politics can deepen divisions and polarize societies along ethnic, racial, religious, or ideological lines.

Example: Political campaigns and policy debates often focus on identity issues, leading to heightened tensions, social fragmentation, and resistance to compromise.

Influence on Policy-Making

Impact: Cultural and identity politics influence policy agendas by prioritizing issues relevant to specific identity groups.

Example: Policies addressing affirmative action, multiculturalism, language rights, and historical injustices reflect identity-based concerns and demands for recognition.

Formation of Political Alliances

Impact: Identity politics fosters coalition-building among diverse identity groups sharing common goals and grievances.

Example: Intersectional movements unite around issues such as environmental justice, healthcare access, and economic equality, leveraging collective power for policy advocacy.

Challenges to National Identity

Impact: Cultural and identity politics challenge traditional notions of national identity, patriotism, and cultural assimilation.

Example: Debates over immigration policies, multicultural education, and national symbols reflect tensions between inclusive diversity and cultural preservation.

Backlash and Resistance

Impact: Identity politics provoke backlash from groups perceiving their interests as marginalized or threatened.

Example: Populist movements and nationalist sentiments often reject multiculturalism, immigration, and diversity initiatives, advocating for policies that prioritize national identity and cultural homogeneity.

Societal Responses and Challenges

Promoting Social Inclusion

Response: Emphasizing inclusive policies, diversity training, and intercultural dialogue to bridge divides and promote understanding.

Challenge: Balancing diverse cultural identities with national unity and social cohesion requires navigating complex historical, political, and socio-economic dynamics.

Navigating Identity-Based Conflicts

Response: Facilitating reconciliation processes, truth commissions, and dialogue initiatives to address historical grievances and promote healing.

Challenge: Resolving identity-based conflicts demands sensitivity, empathy, and commitment to justice, often requiring long-term engagement and community involvement.

Protecting Minority Rights

Response: Strengthening legal protections, anti-discrimination laws, and human rights frameworks to safeguard minority rights and promote equal opportunities.

Challenge: Ensuring effective implementation and enforcement of laws against discrimination and promoting social acceptance of diverse identities remain ongoing challenges in many societies.

Conclusion

Cultural and identity politics play a pivotal role in shaping contemporary societies, influencing public discourse, policy agendas, and societal values. While empowering marginalized groups and advancing social justice, identity politics also pose challenges, including polarization, nationalist backlash, and tensions over national identity. By fostering inclusive dialogue, promoting equitable policies, and respecting diverse cultural identities, societies can navigate identity-based dynamics constructively, promote social cohesion, and uphold human rights in an increasingly diverse and interconnected world.

Migration and refugee crises

Migration and refugee crises have become pressing global issues, driven by factors such as conflict, political instability, economic disparities, climate change, and demographic shifts. These crises pose significant humanitarian challenges and have profound socio-economic and political implications for both host countries and migrants/refugees.

Causes of Migration and Refugee Crises

Conflict and Political Instability

Cause: Armed conflicts, civil wars, persecution, and human rights abuses force people to flee their homes in search of safety.

Impact: Refugee populations swell, straining humanitarian resources and destabilizing regions of origin and neighboring countries.

Economic Hardship and Poverty

Cause: Economic disparities, lack of job opportunities, and poverty drive economic migrants to seek better prospects abroad.

Impact: Economic migration contributes to demographic shifts, labor market dynamics, and socio-economic integration challenges in host countries.

Environmental Factors

Cause: Climate change, natural disasters, and environmental degradation displace populations and contribute to environmental migration.

Impact: Environmental refugees seek refuge in host countries, exacerbating resource competition and environmental stress in receiving communities.

Demographic Pressures

Cause: Population growth, demographic imbalances, and urbanization strain infrastructure and services, prompting internal and international migration.

Impact: Migration flows influence demographic trends, labor markets, and social cohesion, shaping socio-economic landscapes in origin and destination countries.

Socio-Economic and Political Implications

Humanitarian Challenges

Impact: Refugee crises strain humanitarian agencies, host communities, and national infrastructure, requiring emergency aid and long-term support.

Example: Refugee camps, displacement settlements, and humanitarian corridors provide essential services but face funding shortages and capacity constraints.

Integration and Social Cohesion

Impact: Host countries face challenges in integrating migrants and refugees into local communities, addressing cultural differences, and promoting social cohesion.

Example: Policies promoting language acquisition, education, employment, and social inclusion facilitate migrant integration and enhance community resilience.

Political and Security Concerns

Impact: Migration and refugee influxes can fuel political debates, nationalist sentiments, and security concerns over border control and sovereignty.

Example: Refugee policies, asylum procedures, and border management strategies influence public opinion, electoral outcomes, and government responses to migration crises.

Economic Contributions and Challenges

Impact: Migrants and refugees contribute to host country economies through labor participation, entrepreneurship, and cultural diversity.

Example: Labor migration fills skill gaps, supports industries such as healthcare and agriculture, and stimulates local economies through consumption and investment.

Global Responses and Mitigation Strategies

International Cooperation

Response: Strengthening global partnerships, frameworks, and conventions (e.g., UNHCR, Geneva Convention) to protect refugee rights and coordinate humanitarian responses.

Example: Refugee resettlement programs, multilateral aid initiatives, and peacebuilding efforts address root causes of displacement and promote sustainable solutions.

Legal and Policy Frameworks

Response: Developing comprehensive asylum laws, refugee protection policies, and migration management strategies to ensure rights-based approaches and humanitarian assistance.

Example: Refugee status determination, resettlement quotas, and integration policies support refugee rights, promote stability, and uphold international obligations.

Development Assistance and Resilience Building

Response: Investing in development aid, resilience-building programs, and conflict prevention to address socio-economic vulnerabilities and reduce displacement risks.

Example: Sustainable development goals (SDGs), humanitarian aid projects, and community-based initiatives empower local populations, strengthen infrastructure, and promote self-reliance.

Conclusion

Migration and refugee crises are complex global challenges with humanitarian, socio-economic, and political dimensions. Addressing these crises requires concerted efforts, international cooperation, and rights-based approaches to protect refugees, support host communities, and promote sustainable solutions. By addressing root causes, strengthening legal frameworks, and fostering inclusive societies, countries can mitigate the impacts of migration and refugee crises and uphold human dignity, solidarity, and global responsibility in an interconnected world.

Public health challenges and pandemics

Public health challenges, including pandemics, pose significant threats to global health security, economies, and social stability. Understanding the causes, impacts, and responses to pandemics is crucial for mitigating risks, enhancing preparedness, and safeguarding public health worldwide.

Causes of Public Health Challenges and Pandemics

Infectious Disease Outbreaks

Cause: Emergence and spread of infectious diseases such as influenza, Ebola, Zika virus, and novel coronaviruses (e.g., COVID-19).

Impact: Pandemics strain healthcare systems, disrupt economies, and pose serious threats to vulnerable populations, leading to high morbidity and mortality rates.

Antimicrobial Resistance (AMR)

Cause: Overuse and misuse of antibiotics and antimicrobial agents contribute to the development of drug-resistant pathogens.

Impact: AMR undermines treatment effectiveness, increases healthcare costs, and limits treatment options for infectious diseases, exacerbating public health challenges.

Globalization and Travel

Cause: Increased international travel and trade facilitate the rapid spread of infectious diseases across borders and continents.

Impact: Globalization accelerates disease transmission, requiring coordinated international responses to detect, monitor, and contain outbreaks effectively.

Environmental and Climate Factors

Cause: Climate change, deforestation, urbanization, and ecological disruptions influence vector-borne diseases and zoonotic infections.

Impact: Environmental changes alter disease transmission patterns, increase vector populations, and expand geographic ranges of infectious diseases, posing new public health threats.

Socio-Economic and Health Implications

Healthcare System Overload

Impact: Pandemics overwhelm healthcare facilities, personnel, and resources, leading to shortages of medical supplies, hospital beds, and intensive care units.

Example: COVID-19 strained healthcare systems globally, highlighting gaps in pandemic preparedness and response capacities.

Economic Disruption

Impact: Pandemics disrupt supply chains, trade, tourism, and business operations, leading to economic downturns, job losses, and financial instability.

Example: Lockdown measures to contain COVID-19 caused global recessionary impacts, affecting industries and livelihoods worldwide.

Social Disruption and Mental Health

Impact: Pandemic-related restrictions, isolation measures, and fear contribute to social unrest, anxiety, and mental health disorders.

Example: Increased rates of depression, stress, and substance abuse during prolonged public health crises require mental health support and community resilience strategies.

Health Inequities and Vulnerable Populations

Impact: Pandemics exacerbate health inequities, disproportionately affecting marginalized communities, elderly populations, and individuals with pre-existing conditions.

Example: Disparities in access to healthcare, information, and vaccination coverage heighten vulnerability and hinder equitable pandemic response efforts.

Global Responses and Mitigation Strategies

Pandemic Preparedness and Response

Response: Strengthening early warning systems, surveillance networks, and rapid response mechanisms to detect, monitor, and contain infectious disease outbreaks.

Example: Global Health Security Agenda (GHSA), World Health Organization (WHO) International Health Regulations (IHR), and pandemic preparedness frameworks enhance global cooperation and capacity building.

Vaccination and Immunization Programs

Response: Promoting universal access to safe and effective vaccines, vaccination campaigns, and herd immunity to prevent disease transmission.

Example: COVID-19 vaccination efforts demonstrate the importance of vaccine distribution equity, vaccine hesitancy mitigation, and community engagement in achieving immunization goals.

Health System Strengthening

Response: Investing in resilient healthcare infrastructure, workforce training, and medical supply chains to enhance pandemic preparedness and response capabilities.

Example: Building surge capacity, stockpiling medical supplies, and improving diagnostic testing capacities support healthcare systems in managing future public health crises effectively.

International Collaboration and Research

Response: Facilitating collaborative research, data sharing, and scientific innovation to develop treatments, therapies, and diagnostics for emerging infectious diseases.

Example: Global partnerships, research consortia, and public-private collaborations accelerate vaccine development timelines and advance medical breakthroughs in pandemic response efforts.

Conclusion

Public health challenges and pandemics present multifaceted risks to global health security, socio-economic stability, and community well-being. By addressing root causes, strengthening health systems, promoting equitable access to healthcare, and fostering international cooperation, countries can enhance resilience, mitigate health risks, and build sustainable public health infrastructures capable of responding to future pandemics and emerging infectious disease threats effectively. Investing in pandemic preparedness, health equity, and collaborative research efforts is essential for safeguarding public health and advancing global health security in an interconnected world.

Building social cohesion and resilience

Building social cohesion and resilience is essential for fostering inclusive societies, promoting unity amidst diversity, and enhancing community readiness to withstand challenges and crises. This involves strengthening bonds among individuals and communities, promoting mutual support, and addressing socio-economic disparities to ensure equitable opportunities and well-being for all.

Key Strategies for Building Social Cohesion and Resilience

Promoting Inclusive Policies and Practices

Strategy: Implementing policies that uphold human rights, protect minority groups, and promote diversity, equity, and inclusion (DEI).

Impact: Reducing discrimination, fostering a sense of belonging, and enhancing social trust and solidarity within communities.

Strengthening Civic Engagement and Participation

Strategy: Encouraging active citizenship, volunteerism, and community involvement in decision-making processes.

Impact: Empowering individuals and communities to contribute to collective goals, address local challenges, and build consensus on shared values and priorities.

Investing in Education and Lifelong Learning

Strategy: Providing quality education, vocational training, and skills development opportunities for all ages.

Impact: Equipping individuals with knowledge, critical thinking skills, and socio-emotional competencies to navigate societal changes, embrace diversity, and contribute to community resilience.

Promoting Intercultural Understanding and Dialogue

Strategy: Facilitating cross-cultural exchanges, dialogue sessions, and cultural appreciation activities.

Impact: Building bridges across diverse cultural, ethnic, and religious groups, promoting respect for differences, and celebrating shared heritage and values.

Supporting Economic and Social Development

Strategy: Investing in sustainable development projects, job creation initiatives, and social welfare programs.

Impact: Reducing socio-economic inequalities, alleviating poverty, and empowering marginalized communities to participate fully in economic opportunities and social life.

Building Trust in Institutions and Governance

Strategy: Strengthening transparency, accountability, and responsiveness of institutions and public officials.

Impact: Enhancing public confidence in governance, promoting civic engagement, and fostering collective action to address systemic challenges and promote social justice.

Examples of Successful Initiatives

Community Resilience Programs

Example: Resilience-building workshops, disaster preparedness drills, and community-based initiatives to enhance local capacity to respond to natural disasters and emergencies.

Youth Empowerment and Leadership

Example: Youth mentorship programs, leadership academies, and youth councils that empower young people to drive positive change, advocate for their communities, and foster intergenerational dialogue.

Cultural Exchange and Integration

Example: Cultural festivals, art exhibitions, and heritage preservation projects that celebrate cultural diversity, promote mutual understanding, and strengthen social bonds among diverse communities.

Social Cohesion in Urban Planning

Example: Designing inclusive public spaces, affordable housing developments, and mixed-use communities that encourage social interaction, foster a sense of belonging, and promote neighborhood resilience.

Challenges and Considerations

Overcoming Divisive Narratives

Challenge: Addressing polarizing ideologies, misinformation, and prejudice that undermine social cohesion and unity.

Consideration: Promoting empathy, dialogue, and media literacy to counter divisive narratives and build bridges across ideological divides.

Ensuring Equitable Access and Participation

Challenge: Bridging digital divides, language barriers, and socio-economic disparities that limit access to resources and opportunities for vulnerable groups.

Consideration: Implementing targeted interventions, affirmative actions, and inclusive policies to ensure equitable participation and representation in decision-making processes.

Building Long-Term Resilience

Challenge: Sustaining community resilience beyond immediate crises or funding cycles.

Consideration: Investing in capacity-building, leadership development, and institutional partnerships to embed resilience-building practices into long-term planning and community development strategies.

Conclusion

Building social cohesion and resilience requires concerted efforts to promote inclusion, empower communities, and address systemic inequalities. By fostering civic engagement, promoting intercultural dialogue, investing in education and economic opportunities, and strengthening trust in institutions, societies can enhance their capacity to withstand challenges, embrace diversity, and thrive amidst rapid societal changes. Through collaborative efforts and sustained investments in community resilience, countries can cultivate a sense of shared responsibility, solidarity, and collective well-being in building a more resilient and cohesive future for all.

CHAPTER SIX

Technological Disruptions

Advances in AI and automation

Advances in AI (Artificial Intelligence) and automation are transforming industries, economies, and societies at a rapid pace, offering opportunities for efficiency, innovation, and economic growth. These advances are driven by breakthroughs in machine learning, robotics, natural language processing, and other AI technologies, impacting various sectors in profound ways.

Key Advances and Impacts of AI and Automation

Industry and Workforce Transformation

Automation of Routine Tasks: AI-powered automation is replacing repetitive tasks in manufacturing, logistics, and service industries, increasing efficiency and reducing labor costs.

Enhanced Productivity: AI algorithms optimize processes, predict demand, and improve production efficiency, leading to higher output and better resource management.

New Job Roles: While some jobs may be automated, AI also creates new roles in AI development, data science, cybersecurity, and human-machine collaboration.

Healthcare and Biotechnology

Diagnostic Accuracy: AI-driven medical imaging and diagnostic tools improve accuracy in detecting diseases such as cancer, speeding up diagnosis and treatment planning.

Drug Discovery: AI algorithms accelerate drug discovery processes by analyzing vast amounts of biomedical data, predicting drug interactions, and optimizing treatment regimens.

Personalized Medicine: AI enables personalized healthcare interventions based on genetic data, patient histories, and real-time monitoring, enhancing patient outcomes.

Transportation and Logistics

Autonomous Vehicles: AI powers self-driving cars and trucks, promising safer and more efficient transportation systems while raising regulatory and ethical considerations.

Supply Chain Optimization: AI algorithms optimize logistics, inventory management, and route planning, reducing costs and improving delivery efficiency.

Smart Cities: AI-enabled traffic management, energy distribution, and public services enhance urban sustainability and livability.

Finance and Business

Algorithmic Trading: AI algorithms analyze market trends, predict stock performance, and execute trades at high speeds, impacting financial markets globally.

Customer Service: Chatbots and virtual assistants powered by AI improve customer interactions, handle inquiries, and provide personalized recommendations.

Risk Management: AI models analyze data to assess credit risks, detect fraud, and enhance cybersecurity measures in financial institutions.

Education and Learning

Adaptive Learning Platforms: AI-based platforms personalize educational content and assessments, adapting to individual learning styles and pacing.

Virtual Classrooms: AI facilitates remote learning through virtual classrooms, tutoring systems, and interactive simulations, expanding access to education globally.

Skill Development: AI-powered training programs help employees acquire new skills through personalized learning paths and real-time feedback.

Challenges and Considerations

Ethical and Societal Implications

Job Displacement: Concerns about job losses due to automation and AI, particularly in sectors with routine tasks susceptible to automation.

Bias and Fairness: AI algorithms may perpetuate biases in data, affecting decisions in hiring, lending, criminal justice, and other domains.

Privacy and Security: Risks of data breaches, misuse of personal information, and vulnerabilities in AI systems require robust privacy regulations and cybersecurity measures.

Regulatory and Policy Frameworks

Ethical Guidelines: Developing ethical frameworks and guidelines for AI development and deployment to ensure transparency, accountability, and fairness.

Labor Market Adaptation: Investing in reskilling and upskilling programs to prepare the workforce for AI-driven changes and mitigate socioeconomic disparities.

International Cooperation: Collaborating on AI governance, standards, and regulations to address global challenges and ensure responsible AI development.

Human-AI Collaboration

Augmented Intelligence: Promoting human-AI collaboration where AI enhances human capabilities, decision-making, and creativity across various fields.

Trust and Acceptance: Building trust and acceptance of AI technologies through transparency, explainability, and inclusive stakeholder engagement.

Education and Awareness: Increasing public understanding of AI capabilities, limitations, and ethical implications to foster informed debate and policymaking.

Advances in AI and automation present immense opportunities for innovation, economic growth, and societal progress. Addressing challenges effectively requires proactive policies, ethical considerations, and collaborative efforts to ensure AI technologies benefit humanity while mitigating risks and promoting inclusive development.

Cybersecurity threats and digital warfare

Cybersecurity threats and digital warfare represent significant challenges in the modern era, encompassing a wide range of malicious activities aimed at exploiting vulnerabilities in digital systems, networks, and information infrastructures. These threats pose risks to national security, economic stability, privacy, and public safety, requiring robust defenses, international cooperation, and strategic responses to mitigate their impact.

Types of Cybersecurity Threats

Cyberattacks

Malware: Software designed to disrupt, damage, or gain unauthorized access to computer systems, including viruses, ransomware, and trojans.

Phishing: Deceptive emails, messages, or websites used to trick individuals into revealing sensitive information or downloading malicious software.

Denial-of-Service (DoS) Attacks: Overloading a system with traffic to disrupt its availability and functionality, often through botnets or amplification techniques.

Data Breaches

Unauthorized Access: Intrusions into databases or networks to steal sensitive information, such as personal data, financial records, or intellectual property.

Insider Threats: Malicious actions or negligence by insiders, including employees or contractors, compromising data security intentionally or unintentionally.

Cyber Espionage and Warfare

State-Sponsored Attacks: Covert operations by governments or state-affiliated actors to gain intelligence, disrupt critical infrastructure, or influence political outcomes.

Cyber Propaganda: Dissemination of false information or manipulation of social media to influence public opinion, elections, or geopolitical dynamics.

Impacts of Cybersecurity Threats

National Security

Critical Infrastructure: Vulnerabilities in sectors such as energy, transportation, healthcare, and telecommunications pose risks to essential services and national defense.

Military Operations: Cyberattacks targeting defense systems, command and control networks, and military technologies can compromise operational readiness and security.

Economic and Financial Stability

Business Disruption: Costs associated with data breaches, downtime, and recovery efforts impact business continuity, productivity, and market confidence.

Intellectual Property Theft: Loss of proprietary information, trade secrets, and research data undermines innovation, competitiveness, and economic growth.

Privacy and Personal Security

Identity Theft: Unauthorized access to personal information for fraudulent activities, financial exploitation, or impersonation.

Surveillance and Monitoring: Invasive surveillance techniques and breaches of privacy rights through compromised devices or surveillance malware.

Strategies for Cybersecurity and Digital Defense

Cyber Defense Measures

Network Security: Implementing firewalls, encryption, intrusion detection systems (IDS), and multi-factor authentication to protect networks and data.

Endpoint Protection: Securing devices (e.g., computers, smartphones) with antivirus software, patches, and secure configuration practices.

Incident Response and Recovery

Incident Response Plans: Developing protocols for detecting, containing, and mitigating cyber incidents to minimize damage and restore operations swiftly.

Backup and Recovery: Regularly backing up data and systems to facilitate recovery in the event of ransomware attacks, data breaches, or system failures.

International Cooperation

Information Sharing: Collaborating with international partners, government agencies, and cybersecurity organizations to share threat intelligence and best practices.

Norms and Diplomacy: Establishing international norms, treaties, and agreements to address cyber threats, promote responsible behavior, and deter malicious actors.

Capacity Building and Education

Workforce Development: Investing in cybersecurity education, training programs, and professional certifications to build a skilled workforce capable of addressing evolving threats.

Public Awareness: Raising awareness among individuals, businesses, and organizations about cybersecurity risks, best practices, and incident reporting.

Regulation and Compliance

Data Protection Laws: Enforcing regulations (e.g., GDPR, CCPA) to protect personal data, enforce accountability, and impose penalties for non-compliance.

Cybersecurity Standards: Adopting industry standards and certifications (e.g., ISO 27001) to ensure organizations implement robust cybersecurity controls and practices.

Addressing cybersecurity threats and digital warfare requires a comprehensive and adaptive approach that combines technological innovation, policy frameworks, international cooperation, and public awareness. By strengthening defenses, fostering collaboration, and promoting resilience, societies can mitigate risks and safeguard digital ecosystems against evolving cyber threats.

Ethical considerations in technological development

Ethical considerations in technological development are crucial to ensuring that advancements in science and technology benefit humanity responsibly, uphold fundamental rights, and mitigate potential harms. These considerations span various aspects of technological innovation, from AI and biotechnology to cybersecurity and privacy, addressing ethical dilemmas and guiding ethical decision-making in research, development, and deployment.

Key Ethical Considerations in Technological Development

Privacy and Data Protection

Data Privacy: Ensuring individuals have control over their personal data, limiting data collection to necessary purposes, and safeguarding against unauthorized access and misuse.

Surveillance: Balancing security needs with privacy rights, avoiding indiscriminate surveillance, and respecting due process and transparency in surveillance practices.

Bias and Fairness

Algorithmic Bias: Addressing biases in AI and machine learning algorithms that reflect or reinforce societal prejudices based on race, gender, ethnicity, or other characteristics.

Fairness in Decision-Making: Ensuring fairness and transparency in automated decision systems, including those used in hiring, lending, and criminal justice.

Accountability and Transparency

Accountability: Establishing clear lines of responsibility and accountability for the design, deployment, and consequences of technological systems and products.

Transparency: Providing clear explanations of how technologies work, their potential impacts, and ensuring stakeholders understand risks and benefits.

Safety and Reliability

Risk Assessment: Conducting thorough risk assessments to identify potential hazards and mitigate risks associated with new technologies, products, or systems.

Reliability: Ensuring technologies are reliable, resilient to failures, and designed with fail-safe mechanisms to minimize harm in case of malfunction or misuse.

Ethical Use of Technology

Dual-Use Technologies: Considering ethical implications of technologies that can be used for both beneficial and harmful purposes, such as AI, biotechnology, and surveillance technologies.

Weaponization: Ethical considerations in the development and deployment of autonomous weapons, cyber weapons, and other technologies with potential military applications.

Social Impact and Equity

Digital Divide: Addressing disparities in access to technology, digital skills, and internet infrastructure to promote inclusive technological development and bridge the digital divide.

Social Justice: Evaluating how technologies impact marginalized communities, vulnerable populations, and socio-economic inequalities, and mitigating adverse effects.

Environmental Impact

Sustainability: Assessing the environmental impact of technological development, including resource consumption, e-waste management, and carbon footprint.

Green Technologies: Promoting the development and adoption of environmentally friendly technologies and sustainable practices in technological innovation.

Ethical Research Practices

Informed Consent: Respecting autonomy and ensuring informed consent in research involving human subjects, genetic data, and sensitive information.

Animal Welfare: Upholding ethical standards in research involving animals, ensuring humane treatment and minimizing suffering in scientific experiments.

Implementing Ethical Frameworks and Guidelines

Ethics Committees: Establishing ethics committees or review boards to oversee research ethics, assess ethical implications, and provide guidance on ethical practices.

Ethical Guidelines: Developing and adhering to ethical guidelines, codes of conduct, and principles that guide responsible technological development, informed by interdisciplinary collaboration and stakeholder engagement.

Education and Training: Providing education, training, and awareness programs on ethical considerations in technology for researchers, developers, policymakers, and the public.

Regulatory Oversight: Implementing regulatory frameworks and policies that enforce ethical standards, promote responsible innovation, and hold accountable those who violate ethical norms.

By integrating ethical considerations into technological development processes, stakeholders can help mitigate risks, enhance societal trust, and ensure that technological advancements contribute positively to human well-being, equity, and sustainability. Ethical foresight and proactive measures are essential in navigating the complexities and potential impacts of emerging technologies responsibly.

The digital divide and access to technology

The digital divide refers to the gap between individuals, households, businesses, or geographic areas with access to modern information and communication technologies (ICTs) and those without. This divide encompasses disparities in access to the internet, digital devices, skills, and knowledge necessary to effectively participate in the digital economy and society. Addressing the digital divide is crucial for promoting equal opportunities, economic development, education, and social inclusion. Here are key aspects and strategies related to the digital divide and access to technology:

Dimensions of the Digital Divide

Access to Infrastructure

Broadband Access: Disparities in access to high-speed internet infrastructure, particularly in rural and remote areas where connectivity is limited or nonexistent.

Digital Devices: Availability of affordable and reliable digital devices, such as computers, smartphones, and tablets, necessary for accessing online resources and services.

Digital Skills and Literacy

Digital Literacy: Proficiency in using digital tools, navigating online platforms, and critically evaluating information accessed through digital channels.

Technical Skills: Knowledge and skills required for utilizing advanced digital technologies, coding, software development, and cybersecurity practices.

Affordability and Cost

Cost Barriers: Financial constraints preventing individuals or households from purchasing digital devices, subscribing to internet services, or accessing digital content.

Digital Divide in Education: Disparities in access to online learning resources, digital educational tools, and remote learning opportunities, affecting educational outcomes.

Impact of the Digital Divide

Economic Impact

Employment Opportunities: Limited access to digital skills and online job platforms hinders employment prospects, particularly in sectors reliant on digital technologies.

Entrepreneurship: Barriers to accessing e-commerce platforms, digital marketing tools, and online payment systems restrict entrepreneurial opportunities and business growth.

Educational Opportunities

Learning Outcomes: Unequal access to digital resources and online educational platforms exacerbates educational inequalities and impacts academic achievement.

Digital Literacy Gap: Students lacking digital literacy skills may struggle to compete in a digitally-driven economy and society.

Social Inclusion and Equity

Access to Information: Limited access to online information and digital services restricts civic engagement, participation in democratic processes, and access to government services.

Healthcare Access: Barriers to telemedicine services and digital health resources impact access to healthcare information, consultations, and remote medical services.

Strategies to Bridge the Digital Divide

Infrastructure Development

Broadband Expansion: Investing in broadband infrastructure, particularly in underserved rural and remote areas, through public-private partnerships and government initiatives.

Community Networks: Establishing community-based internet access initiatives and Wi-Fi hotspots to provide affordable connectivity in marginalized communities.

Digital Inclusion Programs

Subsidies and Affordability Programs: Providing subsidies, vouchers, or tax incentives to reduce the cost of internet access and digital devices for low-income households.

Digital Literacy Training: Offering training programs, workshops, and educational resources to improve digital literacy skills among individuals of all ages.

Policy and Regulatory Measures

Universal Service Obligations: Implementing policies that mandate universal access to affordable and reliable broadband services as a basic right for all citizens.

Digital Rights: Ensuring regulatory frameworks protect digital rights, privacy, and consumer protections while promoting equitable access to digital resources.

Public-Private Partnerships

Corporate Social Responsibility: Engaging private sector companies in initiatives to provide digital infrastructure, devices, and training to underserved communities.

Tech for Good Initiatives: Collaborating with technology companies and NGOs to develop innovative solutions for bridging the digital divide and promoting digital inclusion.

Research and Data Collection

Data-driven Policies: Conducting research and collecting data on digital divide disparities to inform evidence-based policies and targeted interventions.

Monitoring and Evaluation: Establishing mechanisms to monitor progress, evaluate impact, and adjust strategies to effectively bridge the digital divide over time.

Conclusion

Bridging the digital divide requires a multi-faceted approach involving infrastructure development, digital literacy programs, policy interventions, and collaborative efforts among governments, businesses, civil society, and international organizations. By addressing access barriers and promoting digital inclusion, societies can empower individuals and communities to fully participate in the digital economy, access essential services, and achieve broader social and economic development goals.

Balancing innovation with societal well-being

Balancing innovation with societal well-being is a critical consideration in navigating the rapid advancements and potential impacts of technology, scientific discoveries, and industrial progress on communities, economies, and the environment. This balance requires thoughtful evaluation, ethical foresight, and proactive measures to ensure that innovations contribute positively to human flourishing while mitigating potential risks and addressing societal concerns. Here are key aspects and strategies for achieving this balance:

Principles for Balancing Innovation and Societal Well-being

Ethical and Responsible Innovation

Ethical Frameworks: Developing and adhering to ethical guidelines, principles, and codes of conduct that prioritize human rights, equity, and environmental sustainability in innovation processes.

Responsible Research and Development: Conducting thorough risk assessments, considering potential impacts on stakeholders, and integrating ethical considerations into research and development (R&D) practices.

Stakeholder Engagement and Inclusivity

Community Involvement: Engaging diverse stakeholders, including communities affected by innovations, in decision-making processes to ensure their voices are heard and concerns addressed.

Public Consultation: Conducting transparent and inclusive public consultations on emerging technologies and innovations to foster trust, gather feedback, and inform policy decisions.

Impact Assessment and Mitigation

Risk Assessment: Assessing potential risks and benefits of innovations, including social, economic, environmental, and health impacts, to inform decision-making and mitigate negative consequences.

Precautionary Principle: Applying the precautionary principle to guide decision-making in situations where scientific uncertainty or potential harm exists, prioritizing precaution and prevention.

Regulatory and Policy Frameworks

Regulatory Oversight: Establishing robust regulatory frameworks that balance innovation incentives with protections for public health, safety, privacy, and consumer rights.

Adaptive Regulation: Adapting regulatory approaches to keep pace with technological advancements, ensuring they remain effective, flexible, and responsive to emerging risks and societal concerns.

Education and Awareness

Digital Literacy: Promoting digital literacy and education programs to empower individuals to navigate technological advancements, understand risks, and make informed decisions.

Public Awareness Campaigns: Raising awareness about the societal impacts of innovations, promoting responsible use of technology, and fostering informed public discourse.

Sustainability and Long-term Considerations

Environmental Impact: Integrating sustainability principles into innovation processes to minimize ecological footprints, reduce resource consumption, and promote environmental stewardship.

Long-term Planning: Considering long-term consequences and planning for the sustainable deployment and management of technologies to avoid unintended negative outcomes.

Collaborative and Adaptive Approaches

Multi-stakeholder Collaboration: Fostering partnerships among governments, industry, academia, civil society, and international organizations to address complex societal challenges and promote responsible innovation.

Iterative Learning and Adaptation: Embracing iterative learning and adaptive management approaches to continuously assess impacts, adjust strategies, and enhance societal benefits while minimizing risks.

Conclusion

Achieving a balance between innovation and societal well-being requires a holistic approach that integrates ethical considerations, stakeholder engagement, regulatory oversight, education, and sustainability principles. By prioritizing human values, fostering inclusive decision-making processes, and proactively addressing potential risks, societies can harness the transformative potential of innovation to enhance quality of life, promote equity, and build resilient and sustainable futures for all.

CHAPTER SEVEN

Global Health Threats

Emerging infectious diseases and pandemics

Emerging infectious diseases (EIDs) and pandemics pose significant global health threats, driven by factors such as environmental changes, globalization, and microbial evolution. Understanding the dynamics of EIDs and pandemic outbreaks is crucial for early detection, rapid response, and effective mitigation strategies to protect public health and mitigate socio-economic impacts.

Causes and Factors Contributing to Emerging Infectious Diseases

Zoonotic Transmission

Cause: Transmission of pathogens from animals to humans, facilitated by close contact with wildlife, livestock, and domestic animals.

Example: SARS-CoV-2 (COVID-19) originated from a zoonotic source, likely through intermediate animal hosts, highlighting the risk of spillover events.

Environmental Changes

Cause: Climate change, deforestation, urbanization, and ecological disruptions alter ecosystems, influencing vector habitats and disease transmission dynamics.

Example: Changes in temperature and rainfall patterns impact vector-borne diseases like malaria and dengue fever, expanding their geographic range.

Globalization and Travel

Cause: Increased international travel, trade, and migration facilitate the rapid spread of infectious diseases across borders and continents.

Example: Air travel contributed to the global dissemination of influenza strains during past pandemics, accelerating disease transmission.

Antimicrobial Resistance (AMR)

Cause: Overuse and misuse of antibiotics and antimicrobial agents lead to the emergence of drug-resistant pathogens.

Example: Multi-drug-resistant tuberculosis (MDR-TB) and antibiotic-resistant bacteria pose challenges for treatment and control efforts, complicating infectious disease management.

Socio-Economic and Health Impacts of Pandemics

Healthcare System Strain

Impact: Pandemics overwhelm healthcare facilities, personnel, and resources, leading to shortages of medical supplies, hospital beds, and critical care capacity.

Example: COVID-19 strained intensive care units globally, highlighting vulnerabilities in pandemic preparedness and healthcare infrastructure.

Economic Disruption

Impact: Pandemics disrupt global supply chains, trade, tourism, and economic activities, leading to recessionary impacts, job losses, and financial instability.

Example: Lockdown measures to contain COVID-19 caused economic recessions and exacerbated inequalities, affecting livelihoods and business operations worldwide.

Social and Psychological Stress

Impact: Pandemic-related restrictions, isolation measures, and fear contribute to mental health disorders, stress, and social unrest.

Example: Increased rates of anxiety, depression, and substance abuse during prolonged public health crises highlight the need for mental health support and community resilience.

Global Security Concerns

Impact: Pandemics pose security threats, strain governance systems, and exacerbate political instability and social unrest.

Example: Societal responses to pandemics may include civil unrest, misinformation campaigns, and challenges to public health measures, complicating containment efforts.

Global Responses and Mitigation Strategies

Pandemic Preparedness and Response

Response: Strengthening early warning systems, surveillance networks, and rapid response capabilities to detect, monitor, and contain infectious disease outbreaks.

Example: Global health partnerships, such as the Global Outbreak Alert and Response Network (GOARN) and the Coalition for Epidemic Preparedness Innovations (CEPI), enhance international cooperation and capacity building.

Vaccination and Immunization Programs

Response: Promoting universal access to vaccines, conducting immunization campaigns, and achieving herd immunity to prevent disease transmission.

Example: COVID-19 vaccination efforts demonstrate the importance of vaccine distribution equity, vaccine confidence-building, and global solidarity in pandemic control.

Health System Strengthening

Response: Investing in resilient healthcare infrastructure, workforce training, and medical supply chains to enhance pandemic preparedness and response capacities.

Example: Building surge capacity, stockpiling medical supplies, and improving diagnostic testing capabilities support healthcare systems in managing future public health crises effectively.

Research and Innovation

Response: Advancing scientific research, data sharing, and innovation to develop treatments, vaccines, and diagnostics for emerging infectious diseases.

Example: Collaborative research initiatives, public-private partnerships, and funding support accelerate medical breakthroughs and enhance pandemic response readiness.

Conclusion

Emerging infectious diseases and pandemics present complex challenges to global health security, socio-economic stability, and public well-being. By addressing root causes, strengthening health systems, promoting equitable access to healthcare, and fostering international cooperation, countries can enhance their resilience to pandemics and mitigate the impacts of future infectious disease outbreaks. Investing in pandemic preparedness, research and development, and community engagement is essential for building global health resilience, protecting vulnerable populations, and promoting sustainable development in an interconnected world.

The role of global health organizations and responses

Global health organizations play a critical role in addressing public health challenges, coordinating international responses, and promoting health equity worldwide. Their efforts range from disease surveillance and outbreak response to advocacy for healthcare access, vaccination programs, and capacity building in resource-limited settings. Understanding their roles and responses is crucial for effective global health governance and pandemic preparedness.

Key Global Health Organizations

World Health Organization (WHO)

Role: Leading international authority on public health within the United Nations system, responsible for setting global health standards, coordinating responses to health emergencies, and providing technical assistance to countries.

Response: WHO leads efforts in disease surveillance, pandemic preparedness, vaccination campaigns, and health system strengthening through initiatives like the International Health Regulations (IHR) and Global Vaccine Action Plan (GVAP).

Centers for Disease Control and Prevention (CDC)

Role: U.S.-based national public health institute, internationally recognized for disease control, prevention, and global health security efforts.

Response: CDC collaborates with WHO and other partners to monitor disease outbreaks, conduct research, provide technical expertise, and support countries in strengthening public health capacities.

Global Fund to Fight AIDS, Tuberculosis and Malaria

Role: International financing organization that mobilizes resources to combat HIV/AIDS, tuberculosis (TB), and malaria in low- and middle-income countries.

Response: Global Fund supports prevention, treatment, and care programs, strengthens health systems, and promotes community engagement to reduce the burden of these diseases globally.

Gavi, the Vaccine Alliance

Role: Public-private partnership focused on increasing access to vaccines for children in the world's poorest countries.

Response: Gavi supports vaccine procurement, delivery systems, and immunization campaigns, aiming to prevent outbreaks of vaccine-preventable diseases and improve health outcomes for vulnerable populations.

Roles and Responses in Pandemic and Health Emergency Situations

Disease Surveillance and Early Warning Systems

Role: Monitoring global health trends, detecting disease outbreaks, and providing timely alerts to countries and international partners.

Response: Deploying rapid response teams, conducting epidemiological investigations, and coordinating emergency operations to contain outbreaks and prevent spread.

Capacity Building and Technical Assistance

Role: Strengthening health systems, training healthcare workers, and improving infrastructure to enhance pandemic preparedness and response capabilities.

Response: Providing technical guidance, conducting workshops, and facilitating knowledge exchange to build sustainable public health capacities at national and regional levels.

Vaccination Campaigns and Immunization Programs

Role: Facilitating equitable access to vaccines, promoting immunization coverage, and achieving global health targets for vaccine-preventable diseases.

Response: Supporting vaccine research and development, negotiating vaccine procurement, and implementing immunization strategies to control disease transmission and protect vulnerable populations.

Policy Advocacy and Global Health Diplomacy

Role: Advocating for health equity, promoting evidence-based policies, and fostering international cooperation to address health disparities and achieve universal health coverage.

Response: Engaging with governments, stakeholders, and civil society to shape health agendas, mobilize resources, and advocate for sustainable investments in health systems strengthening.

Challenges and Considerations

Funding and Resource Constraints

Challenge: Securing sustainable financing, mobilizing resources, and prioritizing investments in health emergencies amidst competing global priorities.

Consideration: Strengthening donor commitments, leveraging innovative financing mechanisms, and advocating for increased public and private sector investments in global health security.

Political Will and Coordination

Challenge: Navigating geopolitical tensions, ensuring political commitment to global health goals, and fostering multilateral cooperation in health emergencies.

Consideration: Promoting dialogue, diplomacy, and consensus-building among stakeholders to overcome barriers, enhance trust, and strengthen global health governance frameworks.

Equitable Access and Health Inequities

Challenge: Addressing disparities in healthcare access, vaccine distribution, and health outcomes among vulnerable populations and marginalized communities.

Consideration: Implementing inclusive policies, targeted interventions, and community engagement strategies to reduce health inequities and improve health outcomes for all.

Conclusion

Global health organizations play pivotal roles in addressing public health challenges, responding to health emergencies, and promoting health equity on a global scale. By collaborating with governments, civil society, and international partners, these organizations strengthen health systems, enhance pandemic preparedness, and mitigate the impact of infectious diseases worldwide. Investing in robust health infrastructure, fostering international cooperation, and advancing evidence-based policies are essential for building resilient health systems and achieving sustainable development goals in an interconnected world.

Access to healthcare and medical innovation

Access to healthcare and medical innovation are critical determinants of health outcomes and quality of life worldwide. Addressing barriers to healthcare access, promoting equitable distribution of medical innovations, and advancing healthcare delivery models are essential for achieving universal health coverage and improving global health outcomes.

Barriers to Healthcare Access

Financial Barriers

Issue: High healthcare costs, out-of-pocket expenses, and lack of health insurance coverage limit access to essential medical services and treatments.

Impact: Financial barriers contribute to health disparities, prevent timely healthcare seeking behavior, and exacerbate socio-economic inequalities in health outcomes.

Geographic and Infrastructural Challenges

Issue: Uneven distribution of healthcare facilities, medical professionals, and resources in rural and underserved areas.

Impact: Limited access to healthcare services, longer travel times, and inadequate infrastructure hinder healthcare delivery and patient outcomes.

Health System Capacity and Resource Constraints

Issue: Insufficient healthcare workforce, medical supplies, and diagnostic equipment in resource-limited settings.

Impact: Healthcare system strain, delays in treatment, and compromised quality of care affect patient outcomes and health system performance.

Socio-Cultural and Language Barriers

Issue: Cultural beliefs, language diversity, and healthcare literacy barriers impede effective communication and patient-provider interactions.

Impact: Reduced healthcare utilization, disparities in healthcare outcomes, and challenges in delivering culturally competent care to diverse populations.

Strategies to Improve Access to Healthcare

Universal Health Coverage (UHC)

Strategy: Ensuring all individuals and communities have access to essential health services without financial hardship.

Approach: Implementing health financing reforms, expanding insurance coverage, and reducing out-of-pocket expenses to achieve equitable healthcare access.

Health System Strengthening

Strategy: Investing in healthcare infrastructure, workforce training, and medical supply chains to enhance service delivery and capacity.

Approach: Building resilient health systems, improving healthcare facilities, and deploying telemedicine and digital health solutions to reach underserved populations.

Community Health Initiatives

Strategy: Engaging communities in health promotion, disease prevention, and primary healthcare delivery.

Approach: Establishing community health centers, mobilizing community health workers, and conducting outreach programs to increase healthcare access and empower local communities.

Public-Private Partnerships (PPPs)

Strategy: Collaborating with private sector entities, non-profit organizations, and academia to leverage resources and expertise in healthcare innovation.

Approach: Supporting research and development of new medical technologies, vaccines, and treatments, and promoting affordable access to innovative healthcare solutions.

Role of Medical Innovation in Healthcare Access

Advancements in Medical Technologies

Impact: Innovations in diagnostics, therapeutics, and medical devices improve treatment efficacy, patient outcomes, and healthcare delivery efficiency.

Example: Development of precision medicine, telehealth platforms, and mobile health applications enhance access to specialized care and remote consultations.

Vaccine Development and Immunization Programs

Impact: Research and innovation in vaccine development prevent infectious diseases, reduce disease burden, and contribute to global health security.

Example: Global efforts to develop COVID-19 vaccines and expand immunization coverage highlight the role of innovation in pandemic response and disease prevention.

Affordable and Accessible Healthcare Solutions

Impact: Promoting affordability, scalability, and sustainability of healthcare innovations to ensure equitable access for all populations.

Example: Initiatives to reduce drug costs, negotiate pricing agreements, and promote generic medicine availability enhance access to essential treatments and medications.

Challenges and Considerations

Health Equity and Inclusivity

Challenge: Addressing disparities in healthcare access, treatment outcomes, and health outcomes among vulnerable populations and marginalized communities.

Consideration: Implementing policies, interventions, and regulatory frameworks that prioritize health equity, social justice, and human rights in healthcare delivery.

Regulatory and Ethical Standards

Challenge: Balancing innovation with patient safety, ethical considerations, and regulatory compliance in healthcare product development and deployment.

Consideration: Strengthening regulatory oversight, fostering transparency, and promoting ethical practices to ensure the safety, efficacy, and accessibility of medical innovations.

Sustainable Financing and Resource Allocation

Challenge: Securing sustainable funding, mobilizing resources, and prioritizing investments in healthcare infrastructure, workforce development, and medical innovation.

Consideration: Advocating for increased public and private sector investments, leveraging international partnerships, and optimizing healthcare spending to achieve long-term health system sustainability.

Conclusion

Improving access to healthcare and advancing medical innovation are pivotal for achieving global health goals, promoting health equity, and enhancing quality of life for individuals and communities worldwide. By addressing barriers to healthcare access, investing in health system strengthening, fostering innovation in medical technologies, and promoting equitable distribution of healthcare resources, countries can build resilient health systems, mitigate health disparities, and ensure universal health coverage as a fundamental human right. Through collaborative efforts and sustainable investments in healthcare access and innovation, societies can achieve better health outcomes and improve well-being for all populations in an interconnected world.

Mental health crises and societal impacts

Mental health crises pose significant challenges to individuals, families, communities, and societies, impacting overall well-being, social cohesion, and economic productivity. Understanding the causes, consequences, and responses to mental health crises is essential for promoting mental health resilience, reducing stigma, and improving access to mental healthcare services.

Causes of Mental Health Crises

Psychological and Emotional Stressors

Cause: Life transitions, traumatic events, interpersonal conflicts, and chronic stress contribute to mental health challenges.

Impact: Increased risk of anxiety disorders, depression, post-traumatic stress disorder (PTSD), and substance abuse disorders during periods of crisis.

Social and Economic Disparities

Cause: Socio-economic inequalities, poverty, unemployment, and housing instability exacerbate mental health vulnerabilities.

Impact: Higher prevalence of mental health conditions among marginalized populations, limited access to mental healthcare services, and disparities in treatment outcomes.

Environmental and Cultural Factors

Cause: Cultural norms, societal expectations, discrimination, and stigma surrounding mental illness affect help-seeking behaviors and treatment adherence.

Impact: Barriers to accessing mental healthcare, delayed diagnosis, and social isolation among individuals experiencing mental health crises.

Health System Challenges

Cause: Insufficient mental health resources, workforce shortages, and fragmented care systems hinder timely access to treatment and support services.

Impact: Overburdened healthcare facilities, long wait times for mental health appointments, and gaps in crisis intervention and suicide prevention efforts.

Societal Impacts of Mental Health Crises

Healthcare Burden and Economic Costs

Impact: Increased healthcare utilization, hospitalizations, and emergency department visits related to mental health crises strain healthcare resources and budgets.

Example: Economic costs of untreated mental illness include lost productivity, disability claims, and indirect costs to society.

Family and Social Dynamics

Impact: Mental health crises affect familial relationships, caregiving responsibilities, and social support networks.

Example: Caregiver stress, family conflict, and social withdrawal among individuals experiencing mental health challenges impact overall family functioning and community cohesion.

Educational and Occupational Challenges

Impact: Mental health crises disrupt educational attainment, academic performance, and workforce participation.

Example: Absenteeism, reduced productivity, and job loss due to mental health conditions affect individual career trajectories and economic stability.

Stigma and Discrimination

Impact: Social stigma, stereotypes, and discrimination against individuals with mental illness contribute to social exclusion and barriers to community integration.

Example: Negative attitudes towards mental health conditions hinder disclosure, treatment adherence, and recovery efforts, perpetuating stigma within society.

Responses and Interventions

Promoting Mental Health Awareness and Education

Response: Raising public awareness, reducing stigma, and promoting mental health literacy to foster understanding and empathy.

Intervention: Mental health campaigns, education programs in schools and workplaces, and community outreach initiatives to promote early intervention and support-seeking behaviors.

Enhancing Access to Mental Healthcare Services

Response: Expanding mental health service delivery, integrating mental health into primary care, and ensuring equitable access to treatment options.

Intervention: Telehealth services, mobile crisis teams, and peer support programs to improve access, affordability, and continuity of mental healthcare services.

Crisis Intervention and Support Systems

Response: Developing crisis response protocols, suicide prevention strategies, and crisis stabilization units to provide immediate support and interventions.

Intervention: Crisis hotlines, mobile outreach teams, and community-based crisis intervention programs to address acute mental health needs and prevent escalation of crises.

Advocacy for Policy and Systemic Change

Response: Advocating for policy reforms, funding allocations, and legislative initiatives to strengthen mental health systems and address systemic barriers.

Intervention: Collaborating with policymakers, stakeholders, and advocacy groups to promote mental health parity, improve service coordination, and enhance legal protections for individuals with mental illness.

Conclusion

Mental health crises have profound societal impacts, affecting individuals, families, communities, and economies globally. By addressing root causes, promoting mental health awareness, reducing stigma, and improving access to comprehensive mental healthcare services, societies can enhance resilience, support recovery, and foster inclusive communities. Investing in early intervention, crisis response capabilities, and systemic reforms is essential for mitigating the societal burden of mental health crises and promoting mental well-being as a cornerstone of public health and social policy. Through collaborative efforts and community engagement, societies can create supportive environments that prioritize mental health, empower individuals, and build stronger, more resilient communities for the future.

Preparing for and mitigating health emergencies

Preparing for and mitigating health emergencies requires comprehensive planning, coordination, and readiness across multiple sectors to effectively respond to outbreaks, natural disasters, and other public health crises. Key strategies and considerations include:

Preparing for Health Emergencies

Risk Assessment and Surveillance

Conducting regular risk assessments to identify potential health threats and vulnerabilities.

Strengthening disease surveillance systems to monitor infectious disease trends and early warning indicators.

Emergency Preparedness Plans

Developing and updating emergency response plans at national, regional, and local levels.

Establishing multi-sectoral coordination mechanisms involving healthcare providers, public health agencies, emergency responders, and community stakeholders.

Capacity Building and Training

Building healthcare workforce capacity through training in emergency response protocols, infection control measures, and crisis management.

Conducting simulation exercises and drills to test response capabilities and improve coordination among response teams.

Stockpiling and Supply Chain Management

Maintaining adequate stockpiles of medical supplies, vaccines, antiviral medications, personal protective equipment (PPE), and other essential resources.

Strengthening supply chain logistics to ensure timely distribution and deployment of emergency supplies during health crises.

Public Communication and Risk Communication

Developing clear communication strategies to provide timely and accurate information to the public, healthcare providers, and stakeholders.

Addressing misinformation, promoting preventive measures, and fostering public trust in health authorities and crisis response efforts.

Mitigating Health Emergencies

Early Detection and Rapid Response

Enhancing early detection capabilities through enhanced surveillance, laboratory diagnostics, and reporting systems.

Implementing rapid response protocols to contain outbreaks, isolate cases, and implement infection control measures effectively.

Vaccination and Immunization Campaigns

Implementing comprehensive vaccination strategies to prevent the spread of vaccine-preventable diseases.

Promoting vaccine uptake through community engagement, education campaigns, and outreach to underserved populations.

Healthcare System Strengthening

Strengthening healthcare infrastructure, including healthcare facilities, laboratories, and critical care capacities.

Improving healthcare access, equity, and quality to ensure timely diagnosis, treatment, and care for affected individuals.

International Cooperation and Collaboration

Collaborating with international partners, organizations, and global health agencies to share data, resources, and expertise.

Supporting global health initiatives, research collaborations, and capacity-building efforts to address emerging health threats collectively.

Monitoring and Evaluation

Monitoring and evaluating emergency response efforts to assess effectiveness, identify lessons learned, and implement continuous improvement measures.

Conducting post-event reviews, debriefings, and after-action reports to inform future preparedness and response activities.

Challenges and Considerations

Resource Constraints and Funding

Addressing financial constraints, budget limitations, and competing priorities for healthcare resources and emergency preparedness.

Advocating for sustained funding, resource mobilization, and investments in public health infrastructure and preparedness activities.

Political Will and Governance

Overcoming political challenges, policy gaps, and governance issues that may hinder effective crisis response and coordination.

Promoting political commitment, policy coherence, and inter-agency collaboration to ensure a unified approach to health emergencies.

Community Engagement and Trust

Engaging communities in preparedness efforts, risk reduction strategies, and response activities.

Building trust, addressing cultural beliefs, and promoting transparency in communication to foster community resilience and support.

Conclusion

Preparing for and mitigating health emergencies require proactive planning, robust infrastructure, and coordinated efforts across sectors and borders. By investing in preparedness measures, strengthening healthcare systems, enhancing surveillance capabilities, and fostering international cooperation, societies can enhance resilience, protect public health, and mitigate the impact of health emergencies on individuals and communities. Continuous learning, adaptation, and collaboration are essential for building sustainable health systems and ensuring effective responses to emerging health threats in an interconnected world.

CHAPTER EIGHT

Resource Scarcity

Food security and agricultural challenges

Food security and agricultural challenges are complex issues that encompass ensuring access to safe, nutritious, and sufficient food for all people, while also addressing environmental sustainability, economic viability for farmers, and resilience to climate change and other shocks. These challenges are influenced by factors such as population growth, changing dietary patterns, limited resources, and the impacts of global warming. Here are key aspects and strategies related to food security and agricultural challenges:

Key Challenges in Food Security and Agriculture

Production and Productivity

Sustainable Agriculture: Promoting sustainable farming practices that conserve natural resources, reduce environmental impact, and enhance soil health.

Climate Change: Mitigating the effects of climate change on agriculture through resilient crop varieties, water management strategies, and adaptation measures.

Access and Distribution

Food Access: Ensuring equitable access to nutritious food, particularly in marginalized and food-insecure communities, through affordable pricing and distribution systems.

Food Waste: Addressing food loss and waste throughout the food supply chain, from production and processing to consumption and distribution.

Economic and Social Factors

Rural Development: Supporting smallholder farmers and rural communities with access to markets, financial services, technology, and infrastructure improvements.

Income Inequality: Addressing disparities in income and livelihood opportunities within the agricultural sector to improve economic resilience and food security.

Policy and Governance

Food Policy: Developing and implementing policies that support sustainable agricultural development, food safety standards, and nutrition programs.

Land Use and Tenure: Promoting secure land tenure rights and sustainable land management practices to enhance agricultural productivity and resilience.

Nutrition and Health

Dietary Diversity: Promoting diverse and nutritious diets to combat malnutrition, including micronutrient deficiencies and diet-related diseases.

Food Safety: Ensuring food safety standards and regulations are enforced to protect public health and consumer confidence in food supply chains.

Strategies for Enhancing Food Security and Agricultural Sustainability

Sustainable Agricultural Practices

Agroecology: Promoting agroecological approaches that integrate ecological principles into farming systems, such as organic farming, agroforestry, and integrated pest management.

Precision Agriculture: Adopting technology-driven practices, like precision farming and smart irrigation systems, to optimize resource use and enhance productivity.

Climate Resilience and Adaptation

Crop Diversity: Supporting the conservation and use of crop diversity to enhance resilience to climate variability and pests.

Climate-Smart Agriculture: Implementing practices that reduce greenhouse gas emissions, conserve water, and enhance soil carbon sequestration.

Strengthening Food Systems

Supply Chain Efficiency: Improving efficiency and resilience in food supply chains through better infrastructure, storage facilities, transportation networks, and market access.

Local Food Systems: Supporting local food production and distribution networks to reduce dependency on global supply chains and enhance food security at the community level.

Research and Innovation

Research Investment: Investing in agricultural research, innovation, and technology development to improve crop yields, develop drought-resistant varieties, and enhance agricultural productivity sustainably.

Digital Agriculture: Harnessing digital technologies, such as remote sensing, big data analytics, and blockchain, to improve decision-making, traceability, and transparency in food systems.

Collaboration and Capacity Building

Public-Private Partnerships: Fostering partnerships between governments, private sector entities, academia, and civil society to leverage expertise, resources, and investments in agricultural development.

Farmers' Empowerment: Empowering farmers with knowledge, skills, and resources through extension services, training programs, and farmer cooperatives to enhance productivity and income.

Conclusion

Addressing food security and agricultural challenges requires integrated approaches that prioritize sustainability, resilience, equity, and nutrition. By promoting sustainable agricultural practices, strengthening food systems, investing in research and innovation, and fostering inclusive policies and partnerships, societies can enhance food security, improve livelihoods, and build resilient agricultural systems capable of feeding a growing global population in a changing climate.

Energy crises and the transition to renewable resources

Energy crises and the transition to renewable resources are critical topics in addressing global energy security, environmental sustainability, and mitigating climate change impacts. Energy crises often arise from factors such as geopolitical tensions, supply disruptions, fluctuating oil prices, and dependence on finite fossil fuel reserves. Transitioning to renewable energy sources offers a pathway to reduce reliance on fossil fuels, mitigate greenhouse gas emissions, and enhance energy resilience. Here are key aspects and strategies related to energy crises and the transition to renewable resources:

Key Challenges in Energy Crises and Transition

Energy Security

Dependency on Fossil Fuels: Vulnerability to supply disruptions, price volatility, and geopolitical risks associated with oil, gas, and coal imports.

Infrastructure Resilience: Aging infrastructure, grid reliability challenges, and vulnerabilities to natural disasters or cyber threats impacting energy supply.

Environmental Impact

Climate Change: Greenhouse gas emissions from fossil fuel combustion contributing to global warming, extreme weather events, and environmental degradation.

Air and Water Pollution: Pollution from fossil fuel extraction, processing, and combustion affecting air quality, water resources, and public health.

Economic and Social Factors

Energy Affordability: Ensuring affordable energy access for households, businesses, and industries amidst rising energy costs and economic uncertainties.

Energy Poverty: Addressing energy poverty in developing countries, where access to reliable and affordable energy services is limited.

Technological and Market Barriers

Technological Readiness: Scaling up renewable energy technologies, improving storage capabilities, and integrating variable renewables into energy grids.

Market Dynamics: Overcoming barriers to renewable energy deployment, such as policy frameworks, financing constraints, and competition with subsidized fossil fuels.

Strategies for Transitioning to Renewable Resources

Renewable Energy Deployment

Solar and Wind Power: Expanding deployment of solar photovoltaic (PV) and wind turbines to harness abundant renewable resources for electricity generation.

Hydropower and Geothermal: Leveraging hydropower and geothermal energy for reliable baseload power and regional energy independence.

Energy Efficiency and Conservation

Efficient Technologies: Promoting energy-efficient appliances, buildings, and industrial processes to reduce energy demand and improve overall efficiency.

Demand-Side Management: Implementing demand response programs and smart grid technologies to optimize energy use and balance supply and demand.

Policy and Regulatory Support

Renewable Energy Targets: Setting ambitious targets and incentives for renewable energy deployment, grid modernization, and energy storage development.

Carbon Pricing: Implementing carbon pricing mechanisms, such as carbon taxes or cap-and-trade systems, to internalize environmental costs and incentivize clean energy investments.

Innovation and Research

Research Investment: Funding research and development in renewable energy technologies, energy storage solutions, and grid integration strategies.

Technological Innovation: Supporting innovation in next-generation renewable technologies, including advanced biofuels, hydrogen fuel cells, and floating offshore wind.

International Cooperation and Financing

Global Collaboration: Collaborating on international agreements, initiatives, and partnerships to accelerate renewable energy deployment and share best practices.

Financial Support: Mobilizing public and private sector investments, development aid, and climate finance to support renewable energy projects in developing countries.

Conclusion

Addressing energy crises and transitioning to renewable resources requires a holistic approach that integrates policy frameworks, technological innovation, market incentives, and international cooperation. By prioritizing renewable energy deployment, enhancing energy efficiency, and fostering sustainable development practices, societies can enhance energy security, mitigate climate risks, and achieve a resilient and sustainable energy future for all.

Mineral and resource depletion

Mineral and resource depletion refers to the gradual exhaustion of natural resources, including minerals, metals, fossil fuels, and other essential raw materials, due to extraction, consumption, and insufficient replenishment rates. This phenomenon poses significant challenges to global sustainability, economic stability, and environmental health. Here are key aspects and strategies related to mineral and resource depletion:

Key Challenges in Mineral and Resource Depletion

Finite Resources

Non-Renewable Nature: Most minerals and fossil fuels are finite resources that cannot be replenished within human timescales, leading to eventual depletion.

Extraction Intensity: Increasing demand and extraction rates exacerbate depletion, impacting geological reserves and increasing environmental impacts.

Environmental Impact

Land Degradation: Habitat destruction, deforestation, and ecosystem disruption associated with mining operations and resource extraction.

Water and Air Pollution: Contamination of water bodies and air quality deterioration from mining waste, chemical spills, and emissions.

Economic and Social Factors

Supply Chain Risks: Vulnerability to supply disruptions, price volatility, and geopolitical tensions affecting resource-dependent industries and economies.

Social Conflict: Land rights disputes, displacement of communities, and labor rights issues in resource-rich regions.

Technological and Market Barriers

Technological Limitations: Challenges in accessing deeper deposits, lower-grade ores, and economically viable extraction methods.

Market Dynamics: Fluctuations in commodity prices, global demand shifts, and competition for scarce resources driving geopolitical tensions.

Strategies for Addressing Mineral and Resource Depletion

Resource Efficiency and Circular Economy

Resource Efficiency: Improving resource use efficiency in production processes, product design, and consumption patterns to minimize waste and extend resource lifespan.

Circular Economy: Promoting circular economy principles, such as recycling, reusing materials, and designing products for longevity and easy disassembly.

Sustainable Mining Practices

Environmental Standards: Adhering to stringent environmental regulations, rehabilitation plans, and sustainable mining practices to minimize ecological impacts.

Technological Innovation: Investing in research and development of cleaner extraction technologies, such as green mining techniques and advanced recycling processes.

Diversification and Substitution

Diversifying Supply Sources: Developing alternative sources of critical minerals, exploring deep-sea mining, and expanding recycling initiatives to reduce dependency on finite resources.

Substitution and Innovation: Investing in research on substitutes and technological innovations that reduce reliance on scarce or environmentally damaging materials.

Governance and Policy Frameworks

Regulatory Oversight: Strengthening regulatory frameworks to ensure responsible resource extraction, environmental protection, and community engagement.

International Cooperation: Collaborating on global agreements, initiatives, and standards to promote sustainable resource management, transparency, and fair trade practices.

Public Awareness and Education

Consumer Awareness: Educating consumers, businesses, and policymakers about the importance of sustainable resource management and the impacts of resource depletion.

Capacity Building: Building capacity in resource-rich countries for sustainable resource governance, economic diversification, and inclusive development.

Conclusion

Addressing mineral and resource depletion requires a comprehensive and collaborative approach that integrates resource efficiency, sustainable mining practices, technological innovation, and robust governance frameworks. By promoting responsible resource management, reducing waste, and fostering a transition towards a circular economy, societies can mitigate the impacts of resource depletion, enhance resource security, and promote long-term environmental and economic sustainability.

Global supply chain vulncrabilities

Global supply chain vulnerabilities refer to weaknesses and risks within the interconnected network of production, distribution, and logistics systems that span across countries and regions. These vulnerabilities can disrupt the flow of goods, services, and information, impacting industries, economies, and global trade. Several factors contribute to supply chain vulnerabilities:

Key Factors Contributing to Supply Chain Vulnerabilities

Dependency on Globalization

Complexity and Interdependence: Supply chains are increasingly complex, involving multiple suppliers, manufacturers, distributors, and service providers across different countries and continents.

Geopolitical Risks: Political instability, trade disputes, tariffs, sanctions, and geopolitical tensions can disrupt supply chain operations and affect global trade flows.

Disruptions and Shocks

Natural Disasters: Events such as earthquakes, hurricanes, floods, and pandemics can disrupt production facilities, transportation networks, and ports, leading to supply chain disruptions.

Man-Made Disruptions: Cyberattacks, terrorism, labor strikes, and economic crises can impact supply chain resilience and continuity.

Operational and Logistical Challenges

Inventory Management: Just-in-time inventory practices leave little buffer against disruptions, increasing vulnerability to supply shortages or delays.

Transportation and Logistics: Dependence on efficient transportation networks (air, sea, road, rail) for timely delivery of goods and services, subject to congestion, delays, and capacity constraints.

Technological and Data Risks

Cybersecurity Threats: Vulnerabilities in digital infrastructure, data breaches, and ransomware attacks can disrupt supply chain operations, compromise sensitive information, and lead to financial losses.

Data Management: Inadequate data visibility and information sharing across supply chain partners can hinder real-time decision-making and responsiveness to disruptions.

Strategies to Enhance Supply Chain Resilience

Diversification and Redundancy

Supplier Diversification: Identifying and developing relationships with multiple suppliers in different geographic regions to mitigate dependency risks.

Redundant Capacity: Building redundancy in production facilities, logistics networks, and inventory levels to absorb shocks and maintain continuity.

Risk Assessment and Management

Supply Chain Mapping: Mapping and analyzing supply chain networks to identify vulnerabilities, dependencies, and critical nodes for targeted risk mitigation strategies.

Scenario Planning: Conducting scenario analysis and risk simulations to prepare for potential disruptions and develop contingency plans.

Collaboration and Transparency

Partnership and Collaboration: Strengthening collaboration with supply chain partners, including suppliers, logistics providers, and customers, to enhance communication, agility, and resilience.

Transparency and Visibility: Improving transparency and visibility across the supply chain through digital technologies, IoT sensors, and blockchain to track inventory, monitor shipments, and mitigate risks.

Resilient Infrastructure and Technology

Infrastructure Investments: Investing in resilient infrastructure, transportation networks, and warehousing facilities to enhance operational continuity and capacity during disruptions.

Technology Adoption: Leveraging advanced technologies, such as AI, machine learning, and predictive analytics, to optimize supply chain operations, forecast demand, and mitigate risks.

Regulatory and Policy Support

Regulatory Compliance: Ensuring compliance with regulatory requirements and standards to mitigate legal and regulatory risks that could disrupt supply chain operations.

Government Support: Collaborating with governments to develop policies that support supply chain resilience, trade facilitation, and infrastructure development.

Conclusion

Addressing global supply chain vulnerabilities requires proactive measures, strategic planning, and collaboration among stakeholders to enhance resilience, mitigate risks, and ensure continuity of supply chain operations. By diversifying suppliers, improving transparency, adopting resilient technologies, and fostering collaboration across the supply chain, businesses and governments can better prepare for and respond to disruptions, safeguarding global trade and economic stability.

Sustainable resource management strategies

Sustainable resource management strategies aim to ensure the responsible use, conservation, and equitable distribution of natural resources to meet current and future societal needs while maintaining ecological integrity. These strategies are essential for promoting environmental sustainability, economic prosperity, and social equity. Here are key sustainable resource management strategies:

Key Sustainable Resource Management Strategies

Conservation and Preservation

Protected Areas: Establishing and expanding protected areas, national parks, and reserves to conserve biodiversity, protect ecosystems, and maintain natural habitats.

Wildlife Management: Implementing sustainable wildlife management practices, such as habitat restoration, anti-poaching efforts, and species conservation programs.

Sustainable Agriculture and Forestry

Agroforestry: Integrating trees and crops in agricultural landscapes to enhance soil fertility, biodiversity, and climate resilience while improving farm productivity.

Forest Management: Adopting sustainable forestry practices, including selective logging, reforestation, and forest certification to ensure long-term timber supply and ecosystem health.

Efficient Resource Use and Recycling

Resource Efficiency: Promoting circular economy principles to minimize resource consumption, reduce waste generation, and optimize resource use throughout the product lifecycle.

Recycling and Waste Management: Developing recycling infrastructure, incentivizing recycling programs, and promoting waste reduction strategies to recover valuable materials and reduce landfill waste.

Renewable Energy and Energy Efficiency

Renewable Energy Adoption: Scaling up deployment of renewable energy sources, such as solar, wind, hydropower, and geothermal, to reduce dependence on fossil fuels and mitigate climate change impacts.

Energy Efficiency: Improving energy efficiency in buildings, industries, and transportation sectors through technology upgrades, building codes, and energy management practices.

Water Resource Management

Water Conservation: Implementing water-saving technologies, efficient irrigation practices, and watershed management strategies to sustainably manage freshwater resources.

Water Quality Protection: Preventing pollution, restoring aquatic habitats, and promoting ecosystem-based approaches to ensure clean and safe water supplies for communities and ecosystems.

Sustainable Urban Planning and Infrastructure

Smart Growth: Adopting compact urban development strategies, mixed land-use planning, and green infrastructure to reduce urban sprawl, enhance livability, and minimize environmental impacts.

Green Buildings: Designing and constructing energy-efficient, environmentally friendly buildings that incorporate sustainable materials, passive design principles, and renewable energy technologies.

Community Engagement and Stakeholder Collaboration

Education and Awareness: Raising awareness about sustainable resource management practices, biodiversity conservation, and climate change adaptation among communities, businesses, and policymakers.

Partnerships and Governance: Fostering collaboration among governments, businesses, NGOs, and local communities to develop and implement inclusive policies, regulations, and initiatives that promote sustainable resource use.

Implementing Sustainable Resource Management

Integrated Planning and Policy Development

Integrated Resource Planning: Integrating economic, environmental, and social considerations into resource management planning and decision-making processes.

Policy Instruments: Using regulatory frameworks, market-based incentives, and voluntary agreements to promote sustainable practices, protect natural resources, and support sustainable development goals.

Monitoring, Evaluation, and Adaptive Management

Data Collection and Monitoring: Establishing robust monitoring systems to track resource use, environmental impacts, and progress towards sustainability goals.

Adaptive Management: Using feedback mechanisms and adaptive management approaches to adjust strategies, improve outcomes, and respond to changing environmental and socio-economic conditions.

Innovation and Technology

Research and Development: Investing in research, innovation, and technology transfer to develop sustainable solutions, improve resource efficiency, and address emerging environmental challenges.

Digital Tools: Harnessing digital technologies, such as remote sensing, big data analytics, and geographic information systems (GIS), to enhance decision-making, monitor ecosystems, and manage natural resources effectively.

Conclusion

Sustainable resource management strategies are essential for balancing economic development, environmental protection, and social equity. By integrating conservation efforts, promoting efficient resource use, adopting renewable energy technologies, and engaging stakeholders in collaborative governance, societies can achieve sustainable development goals, enhance resilience to environmental changes, and ensure the well-being of current and future generations.

CHAPTER NINE
Human Rights and Justice

Violations of human rights and international law

Addressing violations of human rights and international law is crucial for promoting justice, upholding dignity, and ensuring accountability on a global scale. Key considerations and responses include:

Types of Violations

Civil and Political Rights Violations

Examples: Arbitrary detention, torture, extrajudicial killings, enforced disappearances, and restrictions on freedom of expression, assembly, and association.

Impact: Denial of due process, suppression of dissent, and infringement of individual liberties and democratic principles.

Social and Economic Rights Violations

Examples: Discrimination, inequality, lack of access to healthcare, education, housing, and basic services.

Impact: Persistent poverty, marginalization, and disparities in opportunities, affecting vulnerable populations and exacerbating socio-economic inequalities.

Violence Against Women and Gender-Based Violence

Examples: Domestic violence, sexual assault, human trafficking, and harmful traditional practices.

Impact: Physical and psychological harm, denial of reproductive rights, and barriers to gender equality and women's empowerment.

Violations in Conflict Settings

Examples: War crimes, genocide, crimes against humanity, and violations of international humanitarian law.

Impact: Loss of lives, displacement of populations, destruction of infrastructure, and long-term socio-economic consequences in conflict-affected regions.

Responses to Violations

Legal and Judicial Mechanisms

Response: Holding perpetrators accountable through national and international legal frameworks, including courts, tribunals, and accountability mechanisms.

Intervention: Prosecuting perpetrators, ensuring fair trials, and seeking justice for victims of human rights abuses and violations of international law.

Diplomatic and Political Engagement

Response: Diplomatic efforts, dialogue, and advocacy to promote human rights, uphold international norms, and address systemic violations.

Intervention: Engaging with governments, international organizations, and civil society to raise awareness, build consensus, and mobilize collective action.

Human Rights Monitoring and Reporting

Response: Monitoring and documenting human rights abuses, violations, and trends through independent investigations and reporting mechanisms.

Intervention: Publishing reports, raising public awareness, and pressuring authorities to take corrective actions to protect rights and prevent further violations.

Capacity Building and Education

Response: Strengthening institutional capacities, training law enforcement officials, judges, and civil servants on human rights standards and legal frameworks.

Intervention: Promoting human rights education, awareness campaigns, and community engagement to empower individuals, promote tolerance, and prevent abuses.

Challenges and Considerations

Impunity and Lack of Accountability

Challenge: Impunity for perpetrators of human rights violations, weak rule of law, and inadequate judicial systems hinder justice and redress for victims.

Consideration: Strengthening legal frameworks, supporting transitional justice processes, and ensuring effective enforcement of international human rights standards.

Political and Security Concerns

Challenge: Political interests, conflicts of interest, and security concerns that undermine efforts to address human rights violations and uphold international law.

Consideration: Balancing political diplomacy with human rights advocacy, promoting dialogue, and leveraging international pressure to influence policy changes.

Protection of Vulnerable Populations

Challenge: Ensuring the protection and rights of vulnerable groups, including refugees, migrants, children, and indigenous peoples, amidst humanitarian crises and displacement.

Consideration: Strengthening protection mechanisms, providing humanitarian assistance, and advocating for inclusive policies that safeguard the rights and dignity of all individuals.

Conclusion

Addressing violations of human rights and international law requires a concerted effort from governments, civil society, international organizations, and global communities. By promoting accountability, strengthening legal frameworks, advancing human rights education, and fostering dialogue, societies can uphold dignity, protect vulnerable populations, and build resilient systems that respect and uphold human rights for all. Continuous advocacy, collaboration, and commitment to justice are essential for addressing systemic challenges, promoting peace, and advancing human rights globally.

The plight of marginalized and vulnerable populations

The plight of marginalized and vulnerable populations remains a critical global concern, marked by systemic inequalities, discrimination, and limited access to essential services. Understanding their challenges and advocating for inclusive policies are crucial steps toward promoting equity and social justice.

Challenges Faced by Marginalized and Vulnerable Populations

Social and Economic Inequality

Challenge: Persistent poverty, unequal distribution of wealth, and barriers to economic opportunities.

Impact: Limited access to education, healthcare, housing, and employment opportunities, perpetuating cycles of disadvantage.

Discrimination and Social Exclusion

Challenge: Prejudice based on race, ethnicity, gender, sexual orientation, disability, or indigenous status.

Impact: Marginalization, stigma, and denial of rights, leading to social exclusion and barriers to full participation in society.

Health Disparities

Challenge: Inadequate access to healthcare services, including preventive care, treatment, and mental health support.

Impact: Higher rates of morbidity and mortality, exacerbated by underlying health conditions and limited healthcare access.

Violence and Human Rights Abuses

Challenge: Exposure to violence, exploitation, trafficking, and human rights violations.

Impact: Physical and psychological trauma, loss of dignity, and challenges in accessing justice and protection.

Environmental and Climate Vulnerability

Challenge: Disproportionate impact of environmental degradation, natural disasters, and climate change on marginalized communities.

Impact: Loss of livelihoods, displacement, and heightened risks to health and well-being in vulnerable regions.

Responses and Interventions

Policy and Advocacy

Response: Advocating for inclusive policies, legal protections, and social safety nets that address systemic inequalities.

Intervention: Promoting anti-discrimination laws, affirmative action policies, and targeted interventions to uplift marginalized groups.

Healthcare Access and Services

Response: Improving access to affordable and culturally competent healthcare services, including reproductive health and mental health support.

Intervention: Strengthening primary healthcare systems, community health initiatives, and outreach programs in underserved areas.

Education and Skills Development

Response: Enhancing access to quality education, vocational training, and lifelong learning opportunities.

Intervention: Providing scholarships, mentorship programs, and skills development initiatives to empower marginalized youth and adults.

Social Protection and Welfare

Response: Establishing social safety nets, including income support, food assistance, and housing programs.

Intervention: Strengthening social security systems, promoting universal healthcare coverage, and ensuring access to basic needs for vulnerable populations.

Community Empowerment and Participation

Response: Promoting community-led development initiatives, participatory decision-making, and grassroots advocacy.

Intervention: Supporting community-based organizations, promoting civic engagement, and amplifying the voices of marginalized groups in policy dialogue.

Challenges and Considerations

Intersectionality and Multiple Marginalizations

Challenge: Recognizing intersecting identities and vulnerabilities that compound discrimination and exclusion.

Consideration: Adopting inclusive approaches that address diverse needs, experiences, and priorities within marginalized populations.

Data and Evidence Gaps

Challenge: Limited data and research on marginalized populations, hindering targeted interventions and evidence-based policy-making.

Consideration: Investing in data collection, research partnerships, and disaggregated data analysis to inform effective interventions and monitor progress.

Political Will and Resource Allocation

Challenge: Prioritizing marginalized populations amidst competing priorities and resource constraints.

Consideration: Advocating for political commitment, resource mobilization, and sustainable funding to address systemic inequalities and support vulnerable communities.

Conclusion

Addressing the plight of marginalized and vulnerable populations requires collective action, political commitment, and systemic reforms to promote equity, justice, and inclusion. By advocating for inclusive policies, enhancing access to essential services, and empowering communities, societies can mitigate disparities, uphold human rights, and build resilient systems that support the well-being and dignity of all individuals, regardless of their background or circumstances. Continuous dialogue, collaboration, and investment in social justice initiatives are essential for creating a more equitable and inclusive world where every person can thrive and contribute to their full potential.

The role of international organizations and NGOs

International organizations and non-governmental organizations (NGOs) play pivotal roles in addressing global challenges, promoting development, advocating for human rights, and responding to humanitarian crises. Their functions, impact, and contributions include:

Roles of International Organizations

Advocacy and Policy Development

Role: Advocating for global norms, standards, and conventions on human rights, humanitarian law, and sustainable development.

Impact: Shaping international agendas, influencing policy decisions, and promoting adherence to principles of justice, equity, and accountability.

Coordination and Collaboration

Role: Facilitating cooperation among member states, NGOs, and other stakeholders to address complex global issues.

Impact: Enhancing collective action, pooling resources, and coordinating responses to humanitarian emergencies, peacebuilding efforts, and development initiatives.

Capacity Building and Technical Assistance

Role: Providing expertise, technical support, and training to build institutional capacities and strengthen governance systems.

Impact: Improving service delivery, enhancing resilience, and promoting sustainable development outcomes in partner countries.

Peacekeeping and Conflict Resolution

Role: Deploying peacekeeping missions, mediation efforts, and conflict resolution initiatives to promote peace and stability.

Impact: Mitigating conflict, protecting civilians, and supporting post-conflict recovery and reconciliation processes.

Humanitarian Assistance and Disaster Response

Role: Delivering emergency aid, relief supplies, and healthcare services to populations affected by natural disasters, conflicts, and humanitarian crises.

Impact: Saving lives, alleviating suffering, and addressing immediate needs while supporting long-term recovery and resilience-building efforts.

Roles of Non-Governmental Organizations (NGOs)

Advocacy and Grassroots Mobilization

Role: Advocating for social justice, human rights, and environmental protection at local, national, and international levels.

Impact: Amplifying marginalized voices, influencing policy outcomes, and promoting civic engagement and participatory democracy.

Service Delivery and Community Empowerment

Role: Providing essential services, including healthcare, education, and livelihood support, to underserved communities.

Impact: Strengthening local capacities, empowering marginalized groups, and fostering sustainable development outcomes.

Monitoring and Accountability

Role: Monitoring human rights violations, governance practices, and implementation of international agreements and conventions.

Impact: Holding governments and institutions accountable, promoting transparency, and advocating for rule of law and good governance.

Capacity Building and Partnership

Role: Building local capacities, fostering partnerships, and promoting collaboration among civil society organizations, governments, and international actors.

Impact: Enhancing organizational effectiveness, promoting knowledge-sharing, and leveraging resources for collective impact.

Innovation and Advocacy

Role: Innovating solutions to emerging challenges, leveraging technology, and promoting inclusive development approaches.

Impact: Driving social change, piloting innovative models, and advocating for inclusive policies that address root causes of poverty, inequality, and injustice.

Challenges and Considerations

Resource Constraints

Challenge: Limited funding, financial sustainability, and resource mobilization for international organizations and NGOs.

Consideration: Diversifying funding sources, strengthening partnerships, and enhancing organizational efficiency to maximize impact and resilience.

Political and Regulatory Challenges

Challenge: Navigating political dynamics, regulatory environments, and restrictions on civil society operations in some countries.

Consideration: Advocating for an enabling environment for civil society, promoting civic space, and engaging in diplomatic dialogue to protect freedoms of expression, association, and assembly.

Coordination and Collaboration

Challenge: Ensuring effective coordination, coherence, and complementarity among diverse stakeholders and actors.

Consideration: Promoting strategic alliances, sharing best practices, and fostering inclusive partnerships to enhance collective action and maximize synergies in addressing global challenges.

Conclusion

International organizations and NGOs play indispensable roles in advancing human rights, promoting sustainable development, and responding to humanitarian crises globally. By leveraging their respective strengths, advocating for inclusive policies, and fostering collaboration across sectors and borders, these organizations contribute to building resilient societies, promoting justice, and achieving shared goals of peace, prosperity, and dignity for all. Continuous support, investment, and engagement with international organizations and NGOs are essential for addressing complex global challenges and creating a more equitable and inclusive world.

Legal frameworks and the pursuit of justice

Legal frameworks are essential for upholding justice, protecting rights, and ensuring accountability within societies. They provide the structure and guidelines through which laws are enacted, interpreted, and enforced to promote fairness and resolve disputes. Key aspects and principles of legal frameworks include:

Elements of Legal Frameworks

Rule of Law

Definition: Principle that all individuals and institutions are subject to and accountable to laws that are fairly applied and enforced.

Role: Upholding fundamental rights, ensuring legal certainty, and promoting accountability in governance and decision-making.

Legal Systems and Jurisdiction

Types: Common law, civil law, Islamic law, customary law, and hybrid systems.

Role: Providing mechanisms for interpreting and applying laws, resolving disputes, and administering justice according to legal traditions and cultural contexts.

Constitutional Law and Human Rights

Role: Establishing foundational principles, rights, and duties of citizens, and delineating powers and responsibilities of government institutions.

Impact: Safeguarding freedoms, protecting minorities, and promoting equality before the law.

Criminal Justice and Due Process

Role: Ensuring fair trials, presumption of innocence, rights of the accused, and adherence to procedural safeguards.

Impact: Preventing arbitrary detention, torture, and ensuring accountability for crimes while protecting the rights of individuals.

Civil Law and Dispute Resolution

Role: Providing mechanisms for resolving civil disputes, enforcing contracts, and protecting property rights.

Impact: Facilitating economic transactions, promoting business confidence, and upholding private rights and obligations.

Pursuit of Justice within Legal Frameworks

Access to Justice

Challenge: Barriers to legal representation, high costs, procedural complexities, and disparities in legal aid services.

Response: Promoting legal empowerment, improving access to courts, alternative dispute resolution mechanisms, and ensuring equitable access to justice for all.

Legal Protections and Safeguards

Challenge: Ensuring enforcement of laws, protection of rights, and addressing impunity for human rights violations.

Response: Strengthening legal institutions, promoting transparency, accountability, and rule of law principles to prevent abuses and ensure accountability.

International Law and Humanitarian Law

Role: Regulating relations between states, protecting human rights, and establishing norms for conflict resolution and humanitarian action.

Impact: Preventing war crimes, genocide, and crimes against humanity, promoting humanitarian assistance, and supporting international cooperation.

Challenges and Considerations

Legal Reform and Capacity Building

Challenge: Outdated laws, gaps in legal frameworks, and institutional weaknesses that hinder effective implementation and enforcement.

Consideration: Undertaking legal reforms, strengthening institutional capacities, and promoting legal education and training to enhance rule of law and governance.

Political Interference and Independence of Judiciary

Challenge: Political influence, corruption, and lack of judicial independence that undermine impartiality and rule of law.

Consideration: Safeguarding judicial independence, promoting accountability mechanisms, and strengthening checks and balances to uphold fairness and integrity in legal processes.

Protection of Vulnerable Groups

Challenge: Ensuring legal protections for marginalized populations, refugees, migrants, and minorities facing discrimination and exclusion.

Consideration: Implementing inclusive legal frameworks, promoting anti-discrimination laws, and addressing systemic barriers to access justice for vulnerable groups.

Conclusion

Legal frameworks form the cornerstone of societies, providing the structure, norms, and mechanisms through which justice is pursued, rights are protected, and disputes are resolved. By upholding rule of law principles, promoting access to justice, and addressing challenges through legal reform and capacity building, societies can strengthen governance, protect human rights, and foster inclusive development. Continuous commitment to transparency, accountability, and respect for the law is essential for promoting justice, upholding rights, and building resilient legal systems that serve the interests and well-being of all individuals and communities.

Promoting human rights and equality

Promoting human rights and equality is fundamental to fostering inclusive societies, upholding dignity, and advancing social justice globally. Key strategies and principles for promoting human rights and equality include:

Principles of Human Rights and Equality Promotion

Universal Declaration of Human Rights (UDHR)

Principle: Recognizes inherent dignity and equal and inalienable rights of all members of the human family as the foundation of freedom, justice, and peace.

Impact: Provides a framework for international human rights law and standards, guiding efforts to protect and promote rights globally.

Non-Discrimination and Equality

Principle: Upholds the principle of non-discrimination based on race, ethnicity, gender, sexual orientation, disability, religion, or other status.

Impact: Promotes equal opportunities, access to resources, and protection against discrimination and marginalization.

Rights-Based Approaches

Principle: Emphasizes that human rights are inherent to all individuals, regardless of nationality, ethnicity, or socio-economic status.

Impact: Guides policies, programs, and interventions to prioritize human dignity, participation, accountability, and empowerment.

Intersectionality

Principle: Recognizes that individuals may experience multiple forms of discrimination and oppression based on intersecting identities.

Impact: Promotes understanding of complex inequalities and informs targeted strategies to address unique challenges faced by marginalized groups.

Strategies for Promoting Human Rights and Equality

Legal and Policy Advocacy

Strategy: Advocating for adoption and implementation of laws, policies, and regulations that protect human rights and promote equality.

Actions: Supporting anti-discrimination legislation, gender equality policies, inclusive education programs, and measures to address socio-economic disparities.

Education and Awareness

Strategy: Promoting human rights education, awareness campaigns, and public engagement initiatives.

Actions: Integrating human rights into school curricula, training programs for civil society organizations, and media campaigns to combat stereotypes and promote tolerance.

Capacity Building and Empowerment

Strategy: Strengthening capacities of individuals, communities, and institutions to claim and defend their rights.

Actions: Providing training on legal literacy, advocacy skills, leadership development, and community organizing to empower marginalized groups and promote civic participation.

Monitoring and Accountability

Strategy: Monitoring human rights violations, documenting abuses, and holding perpetrators accountable.

Actions: Supporting independent human rights institutions, conducting research and reporting on human rights conditions, and advocating for justice and reparations for victims.

Partnerships and Collaboration

Strategy: Building partnerships among governments, international organizations, civil society, and private sector to advance human rights and equality.

Actions: Collaborating on joint initiatives, sharing best practices, and mobilizing resources to address systemic challenges and promote inclusive development.

Challenges and Considerations

Resistance and Backlash

Challenge: Opposition to human rights principles, cultural relativism, and political resistance to rights-based approaches.

Consideration: Engaging in dialogue, building alliances, and promoting inclusive narratives to overcome resistance and advance rights-based agendas.

Resource Constraints

Challenge: Limited funding, capacity gaps, and competing priorities that hinder effective implementation of human rights and equality initiatives.

Consideration: Advocating for resource mobilization, leveraging partnerships, and promoting sustainable funding mechanisms to support long-term human rights promotion efforts.

Intersectional Discrimination

Challenge: Addressing complex intersections of discrimination based on race, gender, disability, sexual orientation, and other factors.

Consideration: Adopting intersectional approaches, conducting inclusive research, and developing targeted interventions to address multiple and intersecting forms of discrimination.

Conclusion

Promoting human rights and equality requires concerted efforts, collaboration, and sustained commitment across all sectors of society. By upholding principles of non-discrimination, empowering marginalized groups, advocating for rights-based approaches, and fostering inclusive policies and practices, societies can create environments where all individuals can live with dignity, equality, and respect for their fundamental freedoms. Continuous advocacy, education, and collective action are essential for advancing human rights, combating discrimination, and building inclusive societies that uphold the rights and well-being of every person.

CHAPTER TEN

The Role of Leadership

Case studies of effective and ineffective leadership

Examining case studies of effective and ineffective leadership provides valuable insights into the qualities, actions, and impacts of leaders in various contexts. Here are examples of both effective and ineffective leadership:

Case Studies of Effective Leadership

1. Nelson Mandela

Context: Nelson Mandela's leadership during South Africa's transition from apartheid to democracy.

Qualities and Actions: Mandela demonstrated resilience, forgiveness, and a commitment to reconciliation. He emphasized inclusivity, brought together diverse factions, and led negotiations that averted civil war.

Impact: Mandela's leadership fostered national unity, reconciliation, and international admiration. He laid foundations for a democratic South Africa and inspired global movements for justice and equality.

2. Indra Nooyi (Former CEO of PepsiCo)

Context: Indra Nooyi's tenure as CEO of PepsiCo, navigating challenges in the beverage and snack industry.

Qualities and Actions: Nooyi prioritized innovation, sustainability, and cultural diversity. She led strategic acquisitions (e.g.,

Tropicana, Quaker) and expanded PepsiCo's healthier product offerings.

Impact: Under her leadership, PepsiCo's revenue and market share grew significantly. She emphasized long-term growth strategies and corporate responsibility, enhancing shareholder value and brand reputation.

Case Studies of Ineffective Leadership

1. The 2008 Financial Crisis - Leadership in Financial Institutions

Context: Leadership failures in major financial institutions contributing to the global financial crisis.

Qualities and Actions: Lack of transparency, risk management failures, and pursuit of short-term profits led to reckless lending and speculative investments.

Impact: The crisis resulted in massive financial losses, bank failures, global economic recession, and widespread public distrust in financial institutions. Regulatory reforms were enacted to prevent future crises.

2. Theranos and Elizabeth Holmes

Context: Elizabeth Holmes' leadership at Theranos, a healthcare technology startup.

Qualities and Actions: Holmes overstated Theranos' capabilities and misled investors, regulators, and customers about the effectiveness of its blood-testing technology.

Impact: The company collapsed amid legal challenges, investigations, and reputational damage. Holmes faced criminal charges for fraud, highlighting the consequences of unethical leadership and deception.

Lessons Learned

Effective leadership is characterized by vision, integrity, adaptability, and a focus on long-term sustainable outcomes. Leaders who inspire trust, foster collaboration, and prioritize ethical decision-making can drive positive change and organizational success. Conversely, ineffective leadership often stems from ethical lapses, poor judgment, lack of accountability, and failure to consider broader consequences.

Angela Merkel

Context: Angela Merkel's leadership as Chancellor of Germany, particularly during the European financial crisis and the refugee crisis.

Qualities and Actions: Merkel demonstrated pragmatism, resilience, and strong leadership in navigating complex challenges. She advocated for European unity, led economic reforms, and managed Germany's response to the refugee influx.

Impact: Merkel's leadership contributed to Germany's economic stability, strengthened European integration, and earned her international respect as a stateswoman.

Satya Nadella (CEO of Microsoft)

Context: Satya Nadella's leadership at Microsoft, leading the company's transformation in the era of cloud computing and artificial intelligence.

Qualities and Actions: Nadella emphasized cultural change, innovation, and customer-centricity. He shifted Microsoft's focus towards cloud services (Azure), AI, and open-source collaboration, revitalizing growth and market relevance.

Impact: Under Nadella's leadership, Microsoft's market value surged, and the company regained its position as a tech industry leader. His inclusive leadership style and strategic vision reshaped Microsoft's culture and business strategy.

More Case Studies of Ineffective Leadership

BP Deepwater Horizon Oil Spill

Context: Leadership failures during the Deepwater Horizon oil spill in 2010, one of the largest environmental disasters in U.S. history.

Qualities and Actions: BP's management overlooked safety protocols, underestimated risks, and prioritized cost-cutting measures over environmental protection. The disaster resulted in a massive oil spill, environmental damage, and loss of lives.

Impact: BP faced severe public backlash, legal penalties, and damage to its reputation. The incident highlighted the consequences of inadequate risk management, regulatory compliance failures, and the importance of responsible corporate leadership.

United Airlines Incident (2017)

Context: Leadership response to a passenger removal incident on a United Airlines flight, which went viral on social media.

Qualities and Actions: United Airlines' management initially mishandled the incident, resulting in public outrage and criticism over customer treatment and crisis management.

Impact: The incident damaged United Airlines' reputation, leading to a decline in stock value and customer trust. It underscored the importance of effective crisis communication, customer-centric policies, and ethical leadership in the airline industry.

Lessons Learned

These case studies illustrate the profound impact of leadership on organizations, communities, and society at large. Effective leaders inspire trust, drive innovation, and navigate challenges with integrity and vision. In contrast, ineffective leadership can lead to crises, reputational damage, and systemic failures. Studying these examples helps identify key leadership principles, ethical considerations, and strategies for fostering positive organizational cultures and societal outcomes.

The qualities and skills of transformative leaders

Transformative leaders possess a unique set of qualities and skills that enable them to inspire, empower, and drive significant change within organizations, communities, and societies. These leaders are often characterized by their visionary outlook, ability to motivate others, and commitment to achieving long-term goals. Here are the key qualities and skills of transformative leaders:

Qualities of Transformative Leaders

Visionary Thinking: Transformative leaders have a clear vision of the future and articulate a compelling direction that inspires others. They envision possibilities, anticipate trends, and set ambitious goals that challenge the status quo.

Courage and Resilience: They exhibit courage to take risks, make tough decisions, and confront adversity. They remain resilient in the face of challenges, setbacks, and criticism, persevering towards their vision.

Integrity and Ethics: Transformative leaders uphold high ethical standards, demonstrate integrity in their actions, and earn trust through transparency and accountability. They prioritize ethical considerations in decision-making.

Empathy and Emotional Intelligence: They possess empathy for others' perspectives, emotions, and needs. They leverage emotional intelligence to build relationships, foster collaboration, and understand the impact of their decisions on stakeholders.

Adaptability and Innovation: Transformative leaders embrace change, adapt to new circumstances, and encourage innovation. They are open to new ideas, experiment with creative solutions, and drive continuous improvement.

Strategic Orientation: They have a strategic mindset, understanding the broader context and implications of their actions. They align organizational goals with their vision and develop strategic plans to achieve transformative outcomes.

Empowerment and Delegation: Transformative leaders empower others by delegating responsibilities, fostering autonomy, and encouraging initiative. They create a supportive environment where individuals can thrive and contribute to collective success.

Collaboration and Inclusivity: They value diversity, promote inclusivity, and build diverse teams. They collaborate across boundaries, seek diverse perspectives, and leverage collective wisdom to drive innovation and achieve shared goals.

Skills of Transformative Leaders

Communication: They are effective communicators who articulate their vision clearly, inspire others through storytelling, and listen actively to diverse viewpoints. They communicate with authenticity and adapt their message to resonate with different audiences.

Decision-Making: They make informed decisions based on data, analysis, and consultation with stakeholders. They weigh risks and benefits, consider long-term consequences, and make timely decisions to advance their vision.

Change Management: Transformative leaders excel in managing change by anticipating resistance, communicating effectively, and engaging stakeholders in the change process. They guide organizations through transitions and foster a culture of resilience.

Conflict Resolution: They navigate conflicts constructively, mediate disputes, and seek win-win solutions. They promote constructive dialogue, address underlying issues, and build consensus to maintain organizational harmony.

Strategic Networking: They build strategic relationships, cultivate networks of influence, and collaborate with key stakeholders. They leverage relationships to gain support for their initiatives, access resources, and drive collective action.

Continuous Learning: Transformative leaders prioritize personal and professional development, continuously learning from experiences, feedback, and insights. They seek knowledge, adapt to changing circumstances, and innovate based on new information.

Responsible Risk-Taking: They assess risks thoughtfully, consider potential impacts, and take calculated risks to drive innovation and growth. They learn from failures, pivot when necessary, and encourage a culture of experimentation.

Impact of Transformative Leadership

Transformative leaders have a profound impact on organizations and societies by fostering innovation, driving growth, and inspiring positive change. They cultivate a culture of trust, engagement, and commitment among followers, empowering individuals to reach their full potential. Through their visionary leadership, they navigate challenges, seize opportunities, and leave a lasting legacy of transformation and sustainable success.

Leadership in times of crisis and uncertainty

Leadership in times of crisis and uncertainty requires a unique blend of qualities, skills, and actions to navigate challenges, provide direction, and instill confidence among stakeholders. Effective leadership during crises involves proactive decision-making, clear communication, empathy, and strategic planning to mitigate risks and guide organizations or communities through adversity. Here are key aspects of leadership in times of crisis and uncertainty:

Qualities of Effective Leadership in Crisis

Calmness and Composure: Leaders maintain a composed demeanor, remaining calm under pressure and reassuring others amid uncertainty. They project confidence and stability to instill trust and inspire confidence.

Resilience and Adaptability: They demonstrate resilience, adapting quickly to changing circumstances, and leading with agility. They anticipate challenges, adjust strategies as needed, and foster a culture of flexibility.

Empathy and Compassion: Effective leaders show empathy towards those affected by the crisis, understanding their concerns, and demonstrating genuine care for their well-being. They communicate empathetically and provide support to individuals and teams.

Transparency and Trustworthiness: They prioritize transparency in communication, sharing accurate information, acknowledging challenges, and addressing concerns openly. They build trust through honesty, accountability, and consistent messaging.

Decisiveness and Accountability: Leaders make timely and well-informed decisions, even amid uncertainty. They take responsibility for their decisions, communicate rationale clearly, and adapt their approach based on feedback and evolving circumstances.

Vision and Strategic Orientation: They maintain a clear vision of long-term goals and objectives, aligning actions with organizational or community priorities. They develop strategic plans to navigate the crisis while preparing for recovery and future resilience.

Skills for Effective Crisis Leadership

Effective Communication: Leaders communicate proactively, clearly, and regularly to keep stakeholders informed and engaged. They use multiple channels and adapt their message to different audiences, addressing concerns and maintaining morale.

Risk Management and Contingency Planning: They assess risks, develop contingency plans, and prioritize actions to mitigate potential impacts. They anticipate scenarios, prepare for worst-case outcomes, and implement measures to enhance resilience.

Collaboration and Team Building: Leaders foster collaboration among teams, stakeholders, and partners to leverage collective expertise and resources. They build cohesive teams, delegate responsibilities, and encourage cross-functional cooperation.

Crisis Response and Decision-Making: They lead crisis response efforts, coordinating resources, and mobilizing teams to execute action plans effectively. They prioritize critical tasks, delegate responsibilities, and monitor progress towards goals.

Ethical Leadership: Leaders uphold ethical principles, making decisions that prioritize the well-being of stakeholders and uphold organizational values. They maintain integrity, fairness, and accountability in all actions and decisions.

Learning and Adaptation: They embrace a learning mindset, seeking feedback, analyzing outcomes, and adapting strategies based on lessons learned. They use data and insights to refine approaches and improve crisis management capabilities.

Strategies for Effective Crisis Leadership

Preparedness and Resilience Building: Leaders invest in preparedness measures, such as crisis simulations, training programs, and infrastructure improvements. They strengthen organizational resilience to anticipate and mitigate future crises.

Stakeholder Engagement and Trust Building: They engage stakeholders proactively, listening to concerns, addressing feedback, and building consensus around crisis response strategies. They cultivate relationships built on trust and transparency.

Innovation and Adaptation: Leaders encourage innovation during crises, exploring new solutions, technologies, and partnerships to address challenges creatively. They promote a culture of innovation that fosters resilience and drives sustainable growth.

Continuous Communication and Updates: They maintain open lines of communication throughout the crisis, providing regular updates, clarifying misinformation, and reinforcing key messages. They use communication to maintain morale and unity.

Post-Crisis Reflection and Improvement: After the crisis subsides, leaders conduct thorough evaluations, assess performance, and identify areas for improvement. They implement changes to strengthen crisis management capabilities and enhance organizational resilience.

Impact of Effective Crisis Leadership

Effective leadership during crises fosters resilience, inspires confidence, and minimizes disruption. It builds trust among stakeholders, enhances organizational or community cohesion, and positions entities for recovery and future success. By demonstrating empathy, making informed decisions, and maintaining strategic focus, leaders can navigate uncertainty, mitigate risks, and lead their organizations or communities towards sustainable resilience and growth.

The impact of leadership on global stability

Leadership plays a crucial role in shaping global stability, influencing geopolitical dynamics, economic resilience, and societal harmony. Effective leadership can promote cooperation, mitigate conflicts, and foster sustainable development, whereas ineffective leadership may exacerbate tensions, economic instability, and social unrest. Here's a detailed exploration of how leadership impacts global stability:

Promoting Cooperation and Diplomacy

International Relations: Leaders can strengthen diplomatic ties, engage in dialogue, and build alliances to resolve disputes peacefully and promote mutual understanding.

Multilateralism: Effective leaders support multilateral institutions and agreements that facilitate cooperation on global challenges such as climate change, health crises, and economic stability.

Mitigating Conflicts and Security Risks

Conflict Resolution: Leaders can mediate conflicts, promote reconciliation, and negotiate peace agreements to reduce violence and promote stability in conflict-prone regions.

Security Policies: Effective leadership in defense and security sectors can enhance national and global security by addressing threats, preventing proliferation, and combating terrorism.

Fostering Economic Stability and Growth

Economic Policies: Leaders influence economic policies that impact global markets, trade relations, and financial stability. Sound economic management can stimulate growth, reduce poverty, and promote sustainable development.

Trade and Investment: Effective leadership promotes fair trade practices, investment in infrastructure, and policies that enhance economic resilience, reducing vulnerabilities to global economic shocks.

Advancing Sustainable Development Goals

Environmental Policies: Leaders can champion environmental sustainability, mitigate climate change impacts, and promote conservation efforts that safeguard natural resources and ecosystems.

Social Development: Effective leadership prioritizes social equity, education, healthcare, and inclusive growth, reducing disparities and enhancing quality of life globally.

Building Resilience to Global Challenges

Pandemic Preparedness: Leadership in public health and crisis management can strengthen healthcare systems, coordinate responses to pandemics, and promote global health security.

Technological Innovation: Leaders can foster innovation, research, and technology transfer that address global challenges such as cybersecurity threats, digital divides, and energy transitions.

Upholding Human Rights and Rule of Law

Human Rights: Leaders uphold human rights, promote rule of law, and combat corruption, fostering societal trust, justice, and respect for fundamental freedoms globally.

Democratic Governance: Effective leadership supports democratic institutions, electoral integrity, and civic participation, reducing political instability and promoting accountable governance.

Influencing Global Norms and Values

Cultural Diplomacy: Leaders promote cultural exchange, diversity, and tolerance, bridging cultural divides and promoting global understanding and cooperation.

Ethical Leadership: Upholding ethical standards, transparency, and accountability enhances trust in leadership and fosters adherence to international norms and conventions.

Case Studies and Examples

Effective Leadership: Nelson Mandela's role in South Africa's transition to democracy promoted reconciliation and stability. Angela Merkel's leadership in the European Union has shaped economic policies and cooperation.

Ineffective Leadership: Leadership failures during conflicts, economic crises, and environmental disasters have exacerbated instability, contributing to humanitarian crises and global challenges.

Conclusion

Leadership significantly influences global stability by promoting cooperation, mitigating conflicts, fostering economic resilience, advancing sustainable development goals, and upholding human rights. Effective leadership fosters trust, enhances international cooperation, and addresses global challenges, contributing to a more stable and prosperous world. Conversely, ineffective leadership can exacerbate divisions, economic instability, and geopolitical tensions, underscoring the critical role of leadership in shaping global outcomes and stability.

Cultivating future leaders for a complex world

Cultivating future leaders for a complex world requires a strategic approach that equips individuals with the skills, knowledge, and mindset to navigate diverse challenges, foster innovation, and drive positive change. Here are key strategies for cultivating future leaders in a complex global landscape:

1. Education and Lifelong Learning

Holistic Education: Emphasize interdisciplinary learning, critical thinking, and problem-solving skills from early education through higher education. Encourage exposure to diverse perspectives and global issues.

Leadership Development Programs: Integrate leadership development into educational curricula, offering courses, workshops, and experiential learning opportunities focused on leadership principles, ethics, and global citizenship.

Continuous Learning: Promote lifelong learning through professional development, mentorship programs, and access to resources that support ongoing growth, adaptation to new technologies, and evolving global trends.

2. Ethical and Inclusive Leadership

Values-Based Education: Instill ethical principles, integrity, and social responsibility as foundational values in leadership development programs. Emphasize empathy, cultural competence, and inclusivity in leadership practices.

Diversity and Inclusion Initiatives: Foster inclusive environments that celebrate diversity of thought, backgrounds, and experiences. Encourage collaboration across diverse teams and promote equity in leadership opportunities.

3. Adaptability and Resilience

Exposure to Complexity: Provide opportunities for future leaders to engage with complex global challenges, such as climate change, technological disruptions, and global health crises. Foster adaptability and resilience in navigating uncertainty and change.

Crisis Management Skills: Offer training in crisis management, risk assessment, and contingency planning to prepare future leaders to effectively lead during emergencies and mitigate impacts on organizations and communities.

4. Global Perspective and Cultural Intelligence

International Experiences: Encourage study abroad programs, international internships, and cross-cultural exchanges to develop global awareness, language skills, and cultural intelligence among future leaders.

Virtual Collaboration Skills: Prepare future leaders for virtual collaboration across borders and time zones. Provide opportunities to work on global projects and initiatives that require understanding and respect for diverse cultural norms and practices.

5. Innovation and Entrepreneurship

Entrepreneurial Mindset: Foster creativity, innovation, and entrepreneurial thinking among future leaders. Encourage experimentation, risk-taking, and the pursuit of novel solutions to societal, economic, and environmental challenges.

Technology Integration: Embrace digital literacy and proficiency in emerging technologies, such as artificial intelligence, blockchain, and data analytics. Equip future leaders to harness technology for innovation and sustainable development.

6. Community Engagement and Social Impact

Service Learning: Promote community engagement and service learning projects that enable future leaders to address local and global social issues. Encourage initiatives that contribute to sustainable development goals and positive social impact.

Corporate Social Responsibility: Integrate principles of corporate social responsibility (CSR) and sustainable business practices into leadership development programs. Empower future leaders to prioritize environmental stewardship and ethical business conduct.

7. Mentorship and Role Models

Role Model Leadership: Provide access to mentorship programs and opportunities for future leaders to learn from experienced professionals and role models. Foster mentor-mentee relationships that support personal growth, leadership development, and career advancement.

Leadership by Example: Encourage current leaders to exemplify ethical leadership, transparency, and accountability. Demonstrate commitment to fostering the next generation of leaders through mentorship, sponsorship, and succession planning.

8. Collaboration with Industry and Government

Partnerships with Stakeholders: Collaborate with industry leaders, government agencies, NGOs, and educational institutions to co-create leadership development programs that address current and emerging global challenges.

Policy Advocacy and Change Management: Equip future leaders with advocacy skills and knowledge of policy-making processes. Prepare them to drive systemic change, influence public policy, and advocate for sustainable development goals at local, national, and global levels.

Conclusion

Cultivating future leaders for a complex world requires a multifaceted approach that integrates education, ethical leadership, adaptability, global perspective, innovation, community engagement, mentorship, and collaboration. By equipping future leaders with these skills and values, we can empower them to navigate complexities, drive positive change, and contribute to a more sustainable, inclusive, and resilient global future.

CHAPTER ELEVEN

Pathways to Resilience

Strategies for building resilient communities and systems

Building resilient communities and systems involves strengthening their capacity to withstand and recover from various shocks, stresses, and challenges. Resilience encompasses social, economic, environmental, and institutional dimensions, aiming to enhance adaptive capacity, reduce vulnerabilities, and promote sustainable development. Here are key strategies for building resilient communities and systems:

Strategies for Building Resilient Communities

Community Engagement and Participation

Strategy: Fostering active participation, inclusive decision-making, and community ownership of resilience-building initiatives.

Actions: Establishing community forums, participatory planning processes, and local committees to identify priorities, share knowledge, and mobilize resources.

Social Cohesion and Inclusion

Strategy: Strengthening social networks, trust, and solidarity among diverse community members.

Actions: Promoting cultural exchanges, intergenerational dialogues, and initiatives that celebrate diversity while addressing inequalities and fostering mutual support.

Education and Awareness

Strategy: Enhancing public awareness, knowledge-sharing, and capacity-building on disaster preparedness, climate resilience, and sustainable practices.

Actions: Integrating resilience education into school curricula, conducting workshops, and leveraging media and technology for information dissemination.

Infrastructure and Environmental Management

Strategy: Investing in resilient infrastructure, sustainable land use planning, and natural resource management.

Actions: Retrofitting buildings for safety, preserving green spaces, promoting water and energy efficiency, and adopting nature-based solutions for climate adaptation.

Economic Diversification and Livelihoods

Strategy: Promoting economic diversification, entrepreneurship, and sustainable livelihood opportunities.

Actions: Supporting local businesses, microfinance initiatives, agricultural diversification, and skills training to enhance economic resilience and reduce dependency on single sectors.

Strategies for Building Resilient Systems

Policy and Governance

Strategy: Strengthening institutional capacities, promoting good governance, and integrating resilience into policy frameworks.

Actions: Developing and implementing resilience strategies, establishing regulatory frameworks, and enhancing coordination among government agencies, private sector, and civil society.

Risk Assessment and Early Warning Systems

Strategy: Enhancing risk assessment capabilities, early warning systems, and decision-support tools.

Actions: Conducting vulnerability assessments, mapping hazards, investing in weather monitoring technologies, and communicating timely alerts to communities and stakeholders.

Healthcare and Social Services

Strategy: Ensuring access to quality healthcare, social services, and psychosocial support during emergencies and crises.

Actions: Strengthening healthcare infrastructure, training healthcare providers in emergency response, and establishing community-based health initiatives.

Technological Innovation and Digital Resilience

Strategy: Harnessing technology, data analytics, and digital platforms to enhance resilience planning and response capabilities.

Actions: Developing mobile apps for disaster alerts, using GIS for spatial planning, deploying drones for damage assessment, and leveraging social media for community engagement.

International Cooperation and Partnerships

Strategy: Fostering collaboration, knowledge exchange, and resource-sharing with international organizations, neighboring countries, and global networks.

Actions: Participating in regional initiatives, joint research projects, and capacity-building programs to address transboundary risks and enhance regional resilience.

Challenges and Considerations

Resource Constraints and Funding

Challenge: Limited financial resources, funding gaps, and competing priorities that hinder investment in resilience-building efforts.

Consideration: Mobilizing public and private investments, exploring innovative financing mechanisms, and advocating for long-term funding commitments to support resilience initiatives.

Climate Change and Environmental Degradation

Challenge: Increasing frequency and intensity of climate-related disasters, ecosystem degradation, and biodiversity loss.

Consideration: Integrating climate adaptation measures, promoting sustainable practices, and enhancing ecosystem resilience to mitigate environmental risks and build ecological resilience.

Community Diversity and Inclusion

Challenge: Addressing diverse needs, preferences, and vulnerabilities within communities, including marginalized and vulnerable groups.

Consideration: Adopting inclusive approaches, respecting cultural diversity, and empowering marginalized populations in resilience planning and decision-making processes.

Conclusion

Building resilient communities and systems requires integrated approaches, collaborative efforts, and sustained commitment from all stakeholders. By investing in community engagement, strengthening infrastructure, enhancing governance, promoting economic diversification, and leveraging technology and innovation, societies can enhance their capacity to adapt, withstand shocks, and thrive in the face of evolving challenges. Continuous learning, adaptation, and inclusive participation are essential for building resilient communities and systems that promote sustainable development, safeguard lives, and ensure a prosperous future for all.

Innovations in sustainability and adaptive technologies

Innovations in sustainability and adaptive technologies are crucial for addressing global environmental challenges, promoting resource efficiency, and enhancing resilience to climate change impacts. These innovations span various sectors and aim to reduce environmental footprints, improve energy efficiency, and foster sustainable practices. Here are some key innovations and technologies driving sustainability and adaptation:

Innovations in Sustainability

Renewable Energy Technologies

Solar Power: Advancements in photovoltaic cells, solar panels, and concentrated solar power (CSP) systems to harness solar energy efficiently.

Wind Power: Innovations in wind turbine design, offshore wind farms, and wind energy storage solutions.

Hydropower: Integration of small-scale hydropower systems and innovative dam designs to minimize ecological impacts.

Energy Storage and Grid Integration

Battery Technologies: Development of high-capacity, low-cost batteries for storing renewable energy and balancing electricity supply-demand.

Smart Grids: Implementation of smart meters, demand response systems, and grid-scale energy storage to optimize energy distribution and efficiency.

Circular Economy Solutions

Resource Recovery: Technologies for recycling, upcycling, and recovering materials from waste streams.

Product Life Extension: Design innovations promoting durability, repairability, and reusability of products to reduce waste generation.

Green Building and Urban Design

Energy-Efficient Buildings: Integration of passive design principles, green roofs, and energy management systems in building construction.

Smart Cities: Adoption of IoT (Internet of Things) sensors, urban data analytics, and sustainable urban planning practices to enhance energy efficiency and livability.

Adaptive Technologies for Climate Resilience

Climate-Resilient Agriculture

Precision Farming: Use of sensors, drones, and data analytics for precision irrigation, nutrient management, and pest control.

Drought-Tolerant Crops: Development of genetically modified crops and traditional crop breeding techniques for resilience to water stress.

Water Management and Conservation

Water Purification: Innovations in water treatment technologies, including desalination, membrane filtration, and decentralized water purification systems.

Water Recycling: Implementation of greywater recycling systems and rainwater harvesting techniques to conserve freshwater resources.

Natural Disaster Preparedness and Response

Early Warning Systems: Development of predictive models, satellite imaging, and mobile apps for timely alerts and evacuation planning.

Resilient Infrastructure: Engineering solutions such as flood barriers, resilient road and bridge designs, and coastal protection structures.

Ecosystem Restoration and Conservation

Natural Climate Solutions: Restoration of wetlands, forests, and mangroves for carbon sequestration and biodiversity conservation.

Bioengineering: Application of bioengineering techniques for shoreline stabilization, erosion control, and habitat restoration.

Challenges and Considerations

Technological Barriers

Complexity: Developing and scaling up technologies that are cost-effective, reliable, and suitable for diverse environmental conditions.

Interdisciplinary Collaboration: Integrating expertise from various fields, including engineering, environmental science, and policy, to address complex sustainability challenges.

Policy and Regulatory Frameworks

Incentives and Support: Establishing supportive policies, incentives for innovation, and regulatory frameworks that promote sustainable technologies and practices.

Standardization: Developing standards and certification processes to ensure safety, efficiency, and environmental sustainability of new technologies.

Access and Equity

Technology Transfer: Bridging the gap between developed and developing countries in accessing and adopting sustainable technologies.

Community Engagement: Ensuring technologies benefit all segments of society, including marginalized communities, and addressing potential social impacts and inequalities.

Conclusion

Innovations in sustainability and adaptive technologies are pivotal for achieving environmental sustainability, enhancing climate resilience, and promoting sustainable development globally. By fostering research and development, fostering collaboration between sectors, and supporting policies that incentivize sustainable practices and technologies, societies can accelerate the transition towards a more resilient, equitable, and sustainable future. Continuous investment in innovation, education, and capacity-building is essential to overcoming challenges and unlocking the full potential of sustainable and adaptive technologies to address pressing global environmental and climate challenges.

The importance of education and awareness

Education and awareness play crucial roles in shaping attitudes, behaviors, and actions towards addressing global challenges, promoting sustainability, and fostering social progress. Here are several key aspects highlighting their importance:

Importance of Education

Knowledge and Skills Development

Role: Equipping individuals with knowledge, skills, and critical thinking abilities necessary to understand complex issues such as climate change, biodiversity loss, and sustainable development.

Impact: Empowering informed decision-making, promoting innovation, and supporting sustainable practices in various sectors.

Behavioral Change and Sustainable Lifestyles

Role: Influencing attitudes, values, and behaviors towards adopting environmentally friendly practices, reducing waste, and conserving natural resources.

Impact: Contributing to lower carbon footprints, promoting recycling and energy conservation, and fostering responsible consumption patterns.

Capacity Building and Empowerment

Role: Building capacities of individuals, communities, and institutions to participate effectively in environmental conservation, climate adaptation, and disaster risk reduction efforts.

Impact: Strengthening resilience, promoting community engagement, and fostering local ownership of sustainable development initiatives.

Global Citizenship and Ethical Responsibilities

Role: Fostering global awareness, empathy, and a sense of responsibility towards addressing global challenges, promoting human rights, and advocating for social justice.

Impact: Cultivating a culture of solidarity, cooperation, and collective action to tackle transboundary issues and promote sustainable development goals.

Importance of Awareness

Public Engagement and Advocacy

Role: Raising public awareness about environmental issues, social inequalities, and human rights violations to mobilize support for policy change and collective action.

Impact: Influencing public opinion, shaping political agendas, and promoting civic engagement in advocating for sustainable policies and practices.

Risk Perception and Preparedness

Role: Increasing understanding of risks associated with climate change impacts, natural disasters, and environmental degradation to foster proactive measures and resilience-building efforts.

Impact: Enhancing community preparedness, improving early warning systems, and reducing vulnerabilities to natural and human-induced hazards.

Cultural Preservation and Heritage Conservation

Role: Promoting awareness of cultural diversity, indigenous knowledge systems, and traditional practices that contribute to sustainable development and biodiversity conservation.

Impact: Safeguarding cultural heritage, promoting intercultural dialogue, and integrating traditional ecological knowledge into modern conservation and development strategies.

Media and Information Dissemination

Role: Leveraging media platforms, digital communication channels, and storytelling to disseminate information, raise awareness, and inspire action on pressing global issues.

Impact: Facilitating knowledge sharing, promoting transparency, and countering misinformation to build public trust and engagement in sustainability efforts.

Challenges and Considerations

Access and Equity

Challenge: Disparities in access to quality education, information, and digital resources, particularly in marginalized communities and rural areas.

Consideration: Promoting inclusive education policies, leveraging technology for remote learning, and addressing socio-economic barriers to ensure equitable access to education and awareness.

Behavioral Change and Long-term Impact

Challenge: Overcoming resistance to change, ingrained consumption patterns, and short-term economic priorities that may hinder sustainable practices.

Consideration: Implementing behavior change campaigns, incentivizing sustainable behaviors, and integrating sustainability into business models and everyday practices.

Collaboration and Partnership

Challenge: Fragmentation of efforts, lack of coordination among stakeholders, and the need for multi-sectoral collaboration in scaling up education and awareness initiatives.

Consideration: Building partnerships across government, civil society, academia, and private sector to leverage resources, share best practices, and amplify impact in advancing education and awareness goals.

Conclusion

Education and awareness are essential catalysts for advancing sustainable development, promoting social equity, and addressing global challenges effectively. By investing in education systems, fostering awareness campaigns, and promoting participatory approaches, societies can empower individuals, mobilize communities, and build the collective resilience needed to achieve a sustainable and inclusive future for all. Continuous commitment to education, awareness, and advocacy is critical for nurturing informed citizens, responsible leaders, and resilient communities capable of addressing current and future global challenges.

Collaborative approaches to global challenges

Collaborative approaches are essential for addressing complex global challenges effectively, as they leverage diverse expertise, resources, and perspectives from multiple stakeholders. Here are key aspects and strategies for fostering collaboration in tackling global challenges:

Key Aspects of Collaborative Approaches

Multi-Stakeholder Engagement

Definition: Involving governments, international organizations, civil society, academia, private sector, and local communities in collaborative efforts.

Role: Harnessing collective strengths, expertise, and resources to address shared challenges and achieve common goals.

Partnerships and Networks

Types: Public-private partnerships (PPPs), cross-sectoral collaborations, global alliances, and regional cooperation frameworks.

Role: Facilitating knowledge sharing, joint initiatives, and coordinated actions to tackle complex issues such as climate change, poverty, and health crises.

Shared Goals and Commitments

Alignment: Establishing common objectives, targets, and timelines through consensus-building and mutual agreement.

Impact: Enhancing accountability, measuring progress, and sustaining momentum towards achieving sustainable development goals (SDGs) and global agendas.

Capacity Building and Empowerment

Capacity: Strengthening institutional capacities, technical expertise, and leadership skills among stakeholders.

Empowerment: Promoting inclusive decision-making, equitable participation, and local ownership of initiatives to ensure sustainable outcomes.

Strategies for Effective Collaboration

Dialogue and Communication

Strategy: Fostering open dialogue, transparency, and mutual understanding among diverse stakeholders.

Actions: Establishing platforms for regular communication, consultations, and information-sharing to build trust and consensus.

Resource Mobilization and Funding

Strategy: Mobilizing financial resources, technical assistance, and in-kind contributions from public, private, and philanthropic sectors.

Actions: Developing innovative financing mechanisms, leveraging public-private partnerships, and aligning investments with sustainable development priorities.

Coordinated Action and Implementation

Strategy: Coordinating activities, leveraging comparative advantages, and avoiding duplication of efforts.

Actions: Developing joint work plans, assigning roles and responsibilities, and monitoring progress through shared indicators and benchmarks.

Policy Harmonization and Advocacy

Strategy: Advocating for policy coherence, harmonization of regulatory frameworks, and alignment with international standards.

Actions: Engaging in policy dialogues, supporting legislative reforms, and advocating for inclusive and equitable policies that promote sustainable development.

Challenges and Considerations

Diverse Perspectives and Interests

Challenge: Balancing divergent priorities, cultural differences, and conflicting interests among stakeholders.

Consideration: Promoting inclusive decision-making processes, facilitating mediation, and fostering mutual respect for diverse viewpoints and priorities.

Sustainability and Long-term Commitment

Challenge: Ensuring sustainability of collaborative efforts beyond short-term projects or funding cycles.

Consideration: Building partnerships based on shared values, mutual benefits, and long-term commitments to achieve lasting impacts and outcomes.

Capacity and Resource Constraints

Challenge: Limited capacities, expertise, and resources, particularly in developing countries and marginalized communities.

Consideration: Providing technical assistance, capacity-building support, and access to innovative technologies to enhance capabilities and empower local stakeholders.

Conclusion

Collaborative approaches are indispensable for addressing global challenges such as climate change, poverty alleviation, and public health crises. By fostering multi-stakeholder engagement, building partnerships, aligning goals and commitments, and overcoming challenges through dialogue and coordinated action, societies can leverage collective strengths and resources to achieve sustainable development, promote social equity, and build resilient communities worldwide. Continuous commitment to collaboration, innovation, and inclusive governance is essential for tackling current and emerging global challenges effectively and creating a better future for all.

Visioning a sustainable and equitable future

Visioning a sustainable and equitable future involves imagining and striving towards a world where environmental sustainability, social equity, and economic prosperity are interconnected and mutually reinforcing. Here's how such a vision can be articulated and pursued:

Elements of a Sustainable and Equitable Future

Environmental Stewardship

Goal: Achieving environmental sustainability by preserving biodiversity, mitigating climate change, and promoting resource efficiency.

Actions: Transitioning to renewable energy sources, promoting circular economy practices, conserving natural habitats, and enhancing ecosystem resilience.

Social Inclusion and Equity

Goal: Ensuring social equity, justice, and inclusion for all individuals and communities, regardless of background or circumstances.

Actions: Addressing inequalities in access to education, healthcare, and economic opportunities; promoting gender equality, and respecting cultural diversity.

Economic Prosperity and Resilience

Goal: Fostering inclusive economic growth, job creation, and sustainable livelihoods that improve quality of life for present and future generations.

Actions: Investing in green technologies and industries, promoting fair trade practices, supporting small-scale enterprises, and enhancing financial inclusion.

Governance and Institutional Integrity

Goal: Promoting accountable, transparent, and effective governance systems that uphold the rule of law and protect human rights.

Actions: Strengthening democratic institutions, combating corruption, promoting civic engagement, and ensuring participatory decision-making processes.

Strategies for Achieving a Sustainable and Equitable Future

Integrated Policy Frameworks

Strategy: Adopting holistic and integrated policy approaches that balance environmental, social, and economic objectives.

Actions: Implementing Sustainable Development Goals (SDGs), integrating climate action into national strategies, and aligning policies across sectors to achieve synergistic outcomes.

Education and Empowerment

Strategy: Empowering individuals and communities through education, awareness, and capacity-building initiatives.

Actions: Promoting environmental literacy, fostering civic engagement, and providing skills training for sustainable practices and entrepreneurship.

Innovation and Technology

Strategy: Harnessing innovation, research, and technology to develop sustainable solutions and adaptive strategies.

Actions: Investing in clean technologies, promoting digital transformation, and supporting research in climate resilience, renewable energy, and sustainable agriculture.

Partnerships and Collaboration

Strategy: Building partnerships across sectors, disciplines, and geographic boundaries to leverage collective strengths and resources.

Actions: Forming public-private partnerships, engaging civil society organizations, academia, and international institutions, and promoting South-South cooperation for knowledge exchange and capacity-building.

Challenges and Considerations

Global Cooperation and Solidarity

Challenge: Addressing global inequalities, geopolitical tensions, and competing national interests that may hinder collective action.

Consideration: Promoting multilateralism, fostering dialogue, and advocating for international cooperation on global challenges such as climate change, migration, and pandemics.

Inclusive Development and Just Transition

Challenge: Managing transitions towards sustainability in ways that minimize social disruption and ensure equitable outcomes for affected communities.

Consideration: Implementing social protection measures, supporting retraining and reskilling programs, and involving stakeholders in planning and decision-making processes.

Long-term Sustainability and Resilience

Challenge: Ensuring resilience to future shocks, including environmental disasters, economic downturns, and health crises.

Consideration: Building adaptive capacities, mainstreaming risk management into development planning, and investing in infrastructure that enhances resilience and sustainability.

Conclusion

A sustainable and equitable future requires bold visions, concerted efforts, and transformative actions at local, national, and global levels. By integrating environmental stewardship, social inclusion, economic prosperity, and good governance into development agendas, societies can pave the way for a resilient, fair, and prosperous future for all. Continuous commitment to innovation, collaboration, and ethical leadership is essential for realizing this vision and ensuring that future generations inherit a planet that is thriving, balanced, and sustainable.

CHAPTER TWELVE

Conclusion and Call to Action

The urgency of addressing global challenges

Addressing global challenges is urgent due to their profound impacts on economies, societies, and the environment worldwide. These challenges are interconnected, spanning from climate change and biodiversity loss to global health crises, inequality, and geopolitical instability. Here are key reasons highlighting the urgency of addressing global challenges:

1. Climate Change and Environmental Degradation

Impact on Ecosystems: Climate change is causing unprecedented shifts in weather patterns, rising sea levels, and increasing frequency of extreme weather events. These changes threaten biodiversity, food security, and freshwater resources.

Economic Costs: Environmental degradation and climate-related disasters impose substantial economic costs through damage to infrastructure, agricultural losses, and healthcare expenditures.

Humanitarian Impact: Displacement of communities due to climate impacts exacerbates social inequalities, poses health risks, and increases vulnerability to natural disasters.

2. Global Health Pandemics

Public Health Threats: Pandemics, such as COVID-19, highlight the interconnectedness of global health systems and the rapid spread of infectious diseases in a globalized world.

Economic Disruptions: Health crises disrupt economies, supply chains, and livelihoods, leading to unemployment, poverty, and economic instability.

Health Equity: Addressing global health challenges requires equitable access to healthcare, vaccines, and public health infrastructure to ensure resilience and preparedness against future pandemics.

3. Inequality and Social Justice

Disparities: Economic inequality, social exclusion, and disparities in access to education, healthcare, and basic services perpetuate poverty and hinder sustainable development.

Human Rights: Upholding human rights, gender equality, and social justice are essential for inclusive development and fostering resilient and cohesive societies.

Conflict and Instability: Social injustices and inequalities contribute to social unrest, conflict, and political instability, undermining peace and security globally.

4. Technological Disruptions and Digital Divides

Digital Transformation: Rapid advancements in technology, such as artificial intelligence and automation, reshape industries, labor markets, and societal norms.

Digital Divide: Unequal access to technology exacerbates inequalities, limiting opportunities for education, employment, and economic participation in underserved communities.

Ethical Considerations: Addressing ethical challenges in technology development, such as privacy concerns, algorithmic bias, and cybersecurity threats, is crucial for responsible innovation and digital governance.

5. Geopolitical Tensions and Global Governance

International Cooperation: Geopolitical tensions, trade disputes, and geopolitical rivalries pose risks to global stability and hinder cooperation on shared challenges, such as climate action and disarmament.

Multilateralism: Strengthening multilateral institutions, international agreements, and diplomatic efforts is essential for addressing global challenges collectively and promoting peace and security.

Rule of Law: Upholding international law, human rights conventions, and norms of responsible governance is critical for resolving conflicts peacefully and advancing global governance.

6. Emerging Risks and Unknowns

Pandemic Preparedness: Building resilience against future health emergencies requires investments in healthcare infrastructure, disease surveillance, and global health security.

Environmental Sustainability: Preserving biodiversity, conserving natural resources, and mitigating climate risks are essential for sustainable development and resilience against environmental shocks.

Future Generations: Addressing global challenges today ensures a sustainable and prosperous future for future generations, safeguarding their rights, opportunities, and quality of life.

Conclusion

The urgency of addressing global challenges stems from their far-reaching impacts on economies, societies, and the environment. By prioritizing cooperation, equity, sustainability, and resilience, we can mitigate risks, foster inclusive development, and build a more just and sustainable world. Acting decisively on these challenges is essential to safeguarding global stability, promoting prosperity, and ensuring a resilient future for all.

The role of individuals, communities, and nations

The role of individuals, communities, and nations is pivotal in addressing global challenges and promoting sustainable development. Each plays a unique but interconnected role in contributing to solutions, fostering resilience, and advancing collective action. Here's how individuals, communities, and nations can contribute:

Individuals

Behavioral Change: Individuals can adopt sustainable lifestyles, reduce carbon footprints, and conserve resources through energy efficiency, waste reduction, and sustainable consumption habits.

Advocacy and Awareness: Individuals can raise awareness about global challenges, advocate for policy changes, and support initiatives that promote environmental sustainability, social justice, and human rights.

Innovation and Entrepreneurship: Individuals drive innovation, entrepreneurship, and technological advancements that address global challenges, such as renewable energy, clean technologies, and healthcare innovations.

Philanthropy and Volunteering: Individuals contribute to global efforts through philanthropic donations, volunteering in community projects, and supporting NGOs and civil society organizations working on social and environmental issues.

Communities

Local Solutions: Communities develop and implement localized solutions to address environmental, social, and economic challenges, tailored to their specific needs and resources.

Collaboration and Partnerships: Communities foster collaboration among stakeholders, including local businesses, educational institutions, NGOs, and government agencies, to implement joint initiatives and maximize impact.

Resilience Building: Communities build resilience against climate impacts, natural disasters, and health crises through community-based adaptation strategies, emergency preparedness, and social safety nets.

Education and Capacity Building: Communities invest in education, skills development, and capacity building to empower residents with knowledge and tools to address local and global challenges effectively.

Nations

Policy and Governance: Nations formulate and implement policies, regulations, and international agreements that address global challenges, such as climate change mitigation, biodiversity conservation, and public health.

Resource Allocation: Nations allocate resources towards sustainable development goals, including investments in renewable energy, infrastructure, healthcare, education, and social welfare programs.

International Cooperation: Nations engage in multilateral diplomacy, collaborate with other countries, and contribute to global initiatives and frameworks that promote peace, security, and sustainable development.

Innovation and Research: Nations support research and innovation in science, technology, and sustainable practices, driving advancements in areas such as agriculture, healthcare, renewable energy, and environmental conservation.

Collaboration Across Scales

Partnerships: Effective collaboration among individuals, communities, and nations fosters synergy, leverages diverse expertise, and scales up impact on global challenges.

Empowerment: Empowering marginalized communities, promoting inclusive decision-making processes, and respecting indigenous knowledge contribute to sustainable development and social justice.

Responsibility: Recognizing shared responsibility and accountability in addressing global challenges ensures equitable outcomes and sustainable development pathways for current and future generations.

Conclusion

Addressing global challenges requires collective action at multiple levels—individuals adopting sustainable practices, communities implementing local solutions, and nations shaping policies and international cooperation. By leveraging their respective roles and responsibilities, individuals, communities, and nations can contribute to building a more resilient, equitable, and sustainable world. Collaboration, innovation, and commitment are essential for achieving global goals and ensuring a prosperous future for all.

Practical steps for immediate and long-term action

Taking practical steps for immediate and long-term action is crucial for addressing global challenges effectively. Whether focusing on environmental sustainability, social justice, economic resilience, or public health, here are actionable steps that individuals, communities, and nations can implement:

Immediate Action

Individuals

Reduce Carbon Footprint:

Immediate: Reduce energy consumption at home, use public transportation, carpool, or switch to electric vehicles.

Long-term: Invest in renewable energy sources, such as solar panels, and support policies promoting clean energy.

Conserve Resources:

Immediate: Reduce water usage, recycle waste, and minimize single-use plastics.

Long-term: Advocate for sustainable consumption habits and support circular economy initiatives.

Support Local Initiatives:

Immediate: Volunteer for community clean-ups, support local farmers markets, and participate in environmental advocacy groups.

Long-term: Advocate for policies that protect local ecosystems, wildlife habitats, and promote sustainable agriculture.

Communities

Community Engagement:

Immediate: Establish community gardens, organize educational workshops on sustainability, and promote recycling programs.

Long-term: Develop community resilience plans for emergencies, such as natural disasters or health crises.

Collaboration and Partnerships:

Immediate: Form alliances with local businesses, schools, and NGOs to address specific community needs, such as affordable housing or food security.

Long-term: Establish sustainable development goals (SDGs) for the community and monitor progress through partnerships with local authorities and stakeholders.

Advocate for Change:

Immediate: Mobilize community members to participate in local governance, advocate for policy changes, and engage in public consultations.

Long-term: Lobby for sustainable urban planning, zoning laws that protect green spaces, and infrastructure investments in renewable energy and public transportation.

Nations

Policy and Legislation:

Immediate: Implement immediate measures to reduce greenhouse gas emissions, enhance environmental protections, and support clean technologies.

Long-term: Ratify international agreements (e.g., Paris Agreement) and develop national strategies for sustainable development across sectors.

Investment in Infrastructure:

Immediate: Allocate funds for resilient infrastructure projects, such as flood defenses, renewable energy installations, and sustainable transport networks.

Long-term: Integrate climate resilience into national development plans, prioritize investments in green infrastructure, and promote sustainable land-use practices.

International Cooperation:

Immediate: Strengthen diplomatic efforts for global collaboration on climate action, disaster response, and pandemic preparedness.

Long-term: Support international development assistance, technology transfer, and capacity-building initiatives to help vulnerable countries adapt to climate change and achieve sustainable development goals.

Long-Term Action

Individuals

Lifestyle Changes:

Long-term: Adopt sustainable diets, reduce personal waste generation, and support ethical consumerism practices.

Continuous Learning: Stay informed about global issues, engage in ongoing education on sustainability, and advocate for environmental justice.

Promote Social Equity:

Long-term: Advocate for equitable access to healthcare, education, and economic opportunities. Support policies that address systemic inequalities and promote social cohesion.

Communities

Resilience and Adaptation:

Long-term: Develop long-term strategies for climate adaptation, disaster risk reduction, and community resilience-building.

Education and Empowerment: Invest in youth leadership programs, mentorship initiatives, and intergenerational dialogue on sustainability and community development.

Innovation and Technology:

Long-term: Foster local innovation hubs, support startups focused on sustainable technologies, and integrate digital solutions for community development and resilience.

Nations

Policy Integration:

Long-term: Integrate sustainable development goals (SDGs) into national policies, budgets, and development plans across sectors.

Monitoring and Accountability: Establish mechanisms for monitoring progress, reporting on environmental and social indicators, and holding accountable those responsible for achieving targets.

Capacity Building:

Long-term: Invest in education, research, and skills development to build national capacity for sustainable development, innovation, and resilience.

International Leadership: Lead by example on global platforms, advocate for ambitious climate action, and collaborate with other nations to address shared challenges.

Conclusion

Taking immediate and long-term action on global challenges requires coordinated efforts at all levels—individuals making sustainable choices, communities implementing local solutions, and nations shaping policies and international cooperation. By prioritizing sustainability, resilience, and equity, we can create a more just, prosperous, and resilient future for generations to come. Collaboration, innovation, and commitment are essential for achieving sustainable development goals and ensuring a thriving planet for all.

Inspiring hope and mobilizing for change

Inspiring hope and mobilizing for change are essential for galvanizing collective action and achieving meaningful progress on global challenges. Whether addressing climate change, social injustice, public health crises, or economic inequality, here are effective strategies to inspire hope and mobilize communities for change:

Inspiring Hope

Communicate Vision and Possibilities:

Storytelling: Share inspiring stories of individuals, communities, and nations making a positive impact through sustainable practices, social justice initiatives, and resilience-building efforts.

Visionary Leadership: Demonstrate commitment to a future where sustainable development, equality, and resilience are achievable goals.

Highlight Progress and Successes:

Celebrate Achievements: Showcase examples of successful projects, innovations, and policies that have led to positive change and improved quality of life.

Empowerment: Empower individuals and communities by highlighting their role in driving change and achieving collective goals.

Educate and Inform:

Raise Awareness: Educate stakeholders about the urgency of global challenges, their interconnected nature, and the potential for transformative change through collective action.

Evidence-based Advocacy: Provide factual information and data-driven insights to underscore the importance and feasibility of solutions.

Mobilizing for Change

Build Coalitions and Partnerships:

Collaborative Networks: Form alliances with diverse stakeholders—NGOs, businesses, governments, and academic institutions—to leverage collective expertise and resources.

Cross-sector Engagement: Engage sectors such as education, healthcare, business, and civil society in collaborative efforts to address complex challenges.

Empower Local Action:

Community Engagement: Empower local communities to lead initiatives tailored to their specific needs and contexts, fostering ownership and sustainability.

Capacity Building: Provide training, resources, and support for grassroots leaders and organizations to implement solutions and drive impact.

Advocate for Policy Change:

Policy Advocacy: Mobilize advocacy efforts to influence policymakers, urging them to adopt and implement policies that prioritize sustainability, social justice, and resilience.

Public Campaigns: Launch public campaigns, petitions, and grassroots movements to raise public awareness and demand political action.

Harness Technology and Innovation:

Digital Engagement: Utilize digital platforms and social media to amplify messages, mobilize supporters, and foster global solidarity around key issues.

Innovative Solutions: Promote technological innovations and scalable solutions that address global challenges effectively and sustainably.

Promote Inclusivity and Diversity:

Inclusive Leadership: Foster inclusive decision-making processes that value diverse perspectives, amplify marginalized voices, and promote social equity.

Empathy and Solidarity: Foster empathy and solidarity across borders and communities, recognizing shared humanity and interconnectedness.

Leading by Example

Commitment to Sustainability:

Corporate Responsibility: Encourage businesses to adopt sustainable practices, transparent governance, and ethical standards in their operations.

Government Leadership: Hold governments accountable for implementing climate action plans, supporting renewable energy transitions, and promoting environmental stewardship.

Education and Youth Engagement:

Empower Youth: Invest in education, leadership development, and mentorship programs to empower youth as agents of change and future leaders.

Schools and Universities: Integrate sustainability education, civic engagement, and social responsibility into curricula to inspire informed and proactive citizenship.

Promote Resilience and Adaptation:

Community Resilience: Support initiatives that build resilience to climate impacts, natural disasters, and health crises, ensuring communities are prepared and adaptive.

Health and Well-being: Prioritize public health, mental well-being, and social safety nets to support vulnerable populations and promote inclusive development.

Conclusion

Inspiring hope and mobilizing for change require visionary leadership, strategic collaboration, and inclusive engagement across sectors and communities. By fostering a sense of optimism, highlighting successes, empowering local action, advocating for policy change, and leveraging technology and innovation, we can collectively address global challenges and create a more sustainable, equitable, and resilient future for all. Each individual's contribution, from grassroots activism to global leadership, plays a crucial role in shaping a world where hope thrives and meaningful change becomes reality.

.....***.....

www.ingramcontent.com/pod-product-compliance
Lightning Source LLC
Chambersburg PA
CBHW071910210526
45479CB00002B/356